TREASURY OF
EGYPTIAN
MYTHOLOGY

CLASSIC STORIES OF GODS, GODDESSES, MONSTERS & MORTALS

BY DONNA JO NAPOLI

ILLUSTRATIONS BY CHRISTINA BALIT

NATIONAL GEOGRAPHIC

WASHINGTON, D.C.

CONTENTS

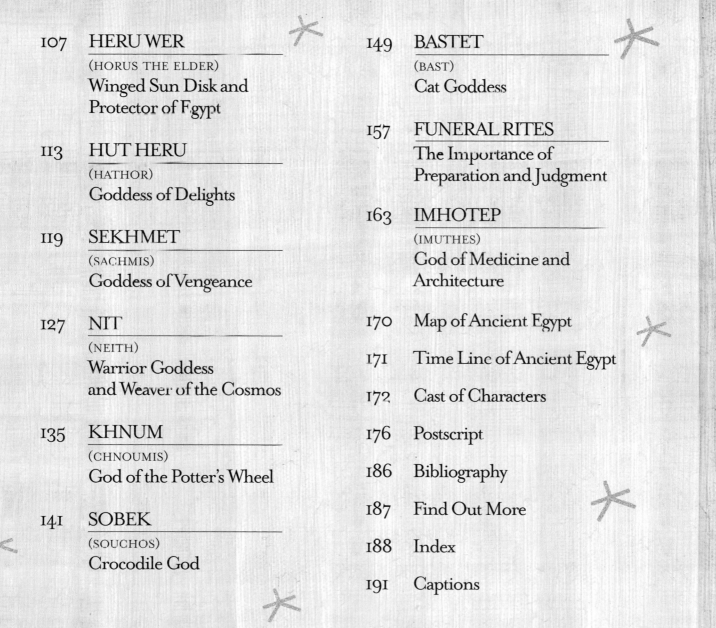

INTRODUCTION

All people count on the sun. It gives them light and warmth. And they count on fresh water, too. Animals and plants need rain, even those that live in the sea, for the sea would grow too salty without it. In modern times, farmers still are concerned with sun and fresh water, because they rely on both to make plants grow, but city people might not think about it much. Our light can be turned on with a wall switch. Our water comes to us through pipes. But in ancient times, sun and fresh water were everyone's concern.

Humans wandered through the Nile valley thousands and thousands of years ago. But around the year 7000 B.C., humans settled there for good. They lived in small, scattered tribes. They foraged and hunted for food, and they raised domesticated animals, such as cows and sheep. In those days Egypt had plenty of grassy land for animals to feed on, especially to the west of the Nile valley, and it also had a mild, wet climate.

But then the climate grew drier. The grasslands known as savannas shrank. Deserts formed. Wild animals had to move close to the Nile shores for water. People followed the animals. Soon towns appeared up and down the riverbanks. And by around 4000 B.C. people turned to farming to produce food. Perhaps there weren't enough plants for foraging anymore. Or perhaps they learned farming from foreigners. Either way, farming meant they could feed lots of people. So towns grew large and stable.

Egyptian farmers relied on three seasons. One season was the flood, when the Nile would overflow its banks. As the floods withdrew, they left behind a muddy substance called silt. Silt is rich in minerals, and it made the soil fertile. Next came the planting and growing season. Finally came the hot and dry harvest season, the time when farmers gathered their crops.

Ancient Egyptian mythology put the sun god Ra in charge of these seasons. After all, his movement across the sky made day and his movement across the underworld made night. Because of his light, crops grew. The very pattern of Egyptian life depended upon Ra.

Egyptian mythology reflects this. Ra is one of the earliest gods, and he remains an important god throughout the long history of ancient Egypt. Most other deities begin somehow from Ra. His tongue, his eye, his saliva, his breath even—they all can step forward as independent gods and goddesses. His thoughts and words create objects and living beings. From his tears came the first humans. Perhaps the Egyptians, then, really believed in only one god—the sun god—who could take many forms.

PREFACE
History of Egyptian Names

I t's hard to know what ancient Egyptians called their gods because they wrote names differently at different times and left out important information. For example, in the earliest hieroglyphs the god Tehuti's name was:

The first symbol, the ibis, is Tehuti's sacred bird. The second is a symbol for the first sound of "top": This shows us that his name started with a *t.* Under that is a symbol for the first sound of "yet." The last is a symbol showing this is a god's name.

By the time of the Old Kingdom (2575–2125 B.C.), the ibis was often replaced by three symbols:

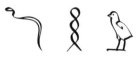

The "snake" stands for the first sound of "June." The "twisted flax" stands for a harsh *h* sound like the one we make when we exhale on glasses before cleaning them, and the "quail chick" stands for the sound(s) following *l* in "glue."

By the Middle Kingdom (2010–1630 B.C.), the first symbol was often replaced with , representing the first sound of "dog." And in the late period (664–332 B.C.) the first symbol was often ∅, perhaps representing the first and maybe second sounds of "tell."

So the initial sound of Tehuti's name changed three times. And linguists argue over what the rest of the sounds in his name were.

When the Greeks invaded, they recorded myths using their alphabet. But Egyptian and Greek did not have exactly the same sounds, so transcribing from one alphabet to the other was only approximate. In addition, Greek spellings were based on more modern pronunciations than those of early Egypt.

For the names in this book, I chose to use the older Egyptian names, not filtered through Greek: hence Tehuti. Nevertheless, I call the country "Egypt" instead of the hardly known ancient name Kemet. And since the Greek names are more familiar, I provide a reference chart below and list the gods' and goddesses' names both ways in the Table of Contents and on the opening pages of each chapter.

Egyptian Name	Greek Name	Egyptian Name	Greek Name
Ra	Helios	Heru Wer	Horus the Elder
Set	Seth	Hut Heru	Hathor
Aset	Isis	Sekhmet	Sachmis
Usir	Osiris	Nit	Neith
Nebet Hut	Nephthys	Khnum	Chnoumis
Heru Sa Aset	Horus the Younger	Sobek	Souchos
Inpu	Anubis	Bastet	Bast
Tefnut	Tphenis	Imhotep	Imuthes
Tehuti	Thoth		

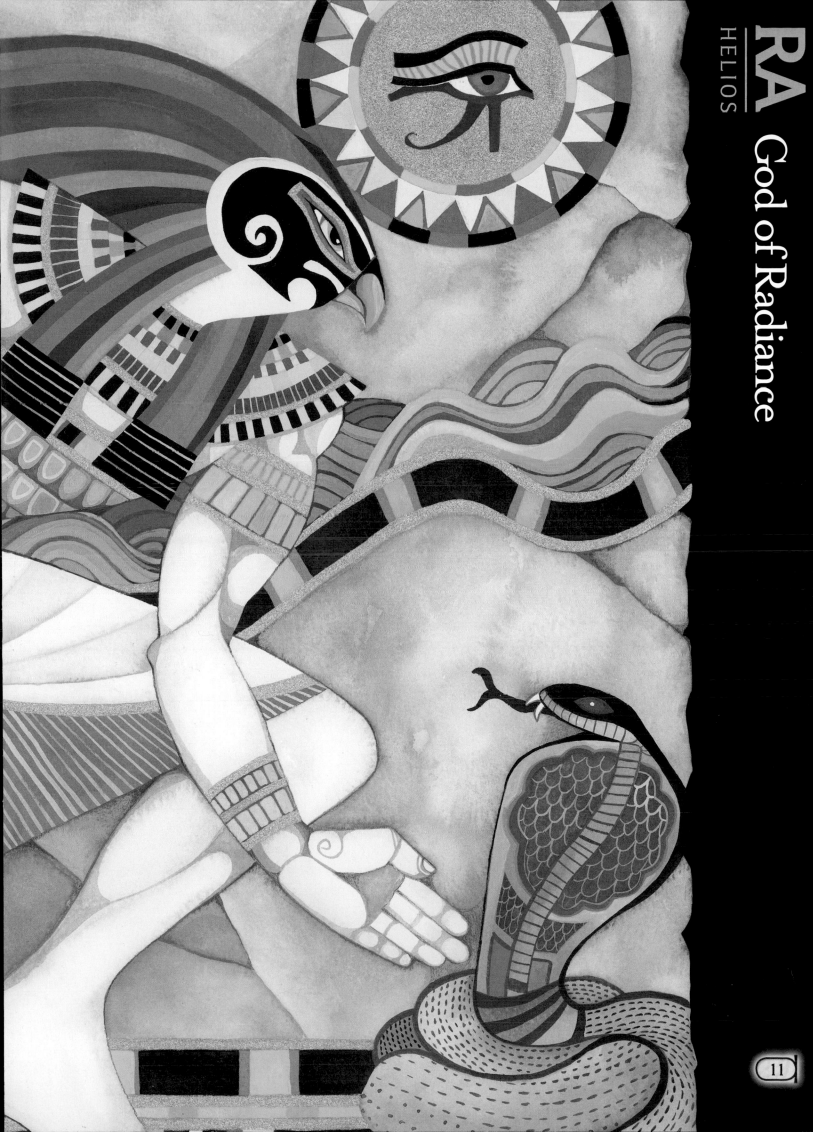

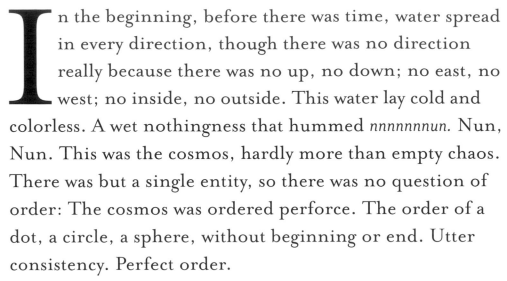

RA (HELIOS)
God of Radiance

In the beginning, before there was time, water spread in every direction, though there was no direction really because there was no up, no down; no east, no west; no inside, no outside. This water lay cold and colorless. A wet nothingness that hummed *nnnnnnnun.* Nun, Nun. This was the cosmos, hardly more than empty chaos. There was but a single entity, so there was no question of order: The cosmos was ordered perforce. The order of a dot, a circle, a sphere, without beginning or end. Utter consistency. Perfect order.

But something there is that doesn't like order. Order can be tolerated temporarily, but on and on like that? Infinite order? How unutterably intolerable. Boring, really.

A hint came. A slight poke. Then another, a little firmer. A full-fledged beat now. More of them. Insistent beats, breaking up the hum, moving the water imperceptibly at first, then in tiny waves, then bigger ones, huge ones now, tsunamis, yet still in a pattern, still ordered, one after another at regular intervals. *Thump thump thump thump.*

A heart formed around this pulse, for every rhythm evokes an origin.

And in that heart nestled a thought. After all, some think with the head and others think with the heart. This was definitely a heart thought.

Ah, the first and the profound disorder: thought.

Language: The True Origin

Most life-forms require water. So it makes sense that Egyptian tales of creation involve a huge water mass. What is striking here, though, is the importance of words, reminiscent of the Bible's Book of John: "In the beginning was the Word." Today many scientists would argue that humanity really started with the development of language. Perhaps the ancients were focusing not so much on the creation of life as on the creation of humans.

A strong ocean wave at sunset illustrates the majesty and power of water.

This single thought rubbed fast and faster until it warmed and finally ignited into language. The god Ra sprang to life with a word already in his mouth. More bubbled up. Words now crowded his mouth. They trampled his tongue and pushed against his teeth, his lips. He had so many words to enunciate. The need hammered at him. From that very need came lungs and a voice box and muscles to make it all move. Ra shouted the first word, over and over, and those shouts rose in molten mass up and up and spewed forth through the waters of Nun in a fiery explosion.

That was the first firmament, the mound of creation that Ra called *benben*—it all started with a single tip, like a volcano mouth. Ra stood upon it in triumph and knew he must speak more. For in his voice lay all creation. He must create, he must never stop creating.

Ra spat and the moisture from within him formed the goddess Tefnut, and the breathy force that propelled that moisture formed the god Shu. The products of his new mouth, his new lungs.

So there were three of them now, three deities distinct from the vast wallow of Nun. It felt wonderful to be a triad; it felt sturdy, invincible even. With three backs together, you could face everything at once. With three, you could explore the three dimensions simultaneously. Though there was no music yet, though there were no colors yet, Ra sensed the possibilities of three at some level he was not yet ready to understand.

But even more than the possibilities was the reality. Life mattered. And being a father mattered. Ra rejoiced in his self-creation. He rejoiced in his creation of his daughter and son. This was a good beginning. Ah, what water had yielded. Ah, indeed.

Ra, his spittle-born daughter Tefnut, and his breath-born son Shu, mingle as one and as three at the same time. They form the first of many triads among the Egyptian gods.

Shu and Tefnut, these royal children, played constantly. They stalked each other and pounced and wrestled. They rolled

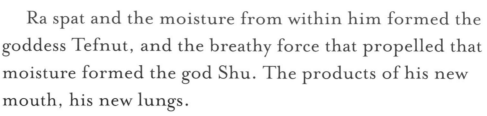

RA (HELIOS)

around and swatted each other. They were like lion cubs, and Ra was like a huge patient lion father, posing contentedly as they chased his tail or combed his mane, though of course there were no lions yet. There were only Shu and Tefnut and Ra, and the vast spreading Nun around the island the triad roamed.

One night, instead of sleeping, Shu and Tefnut went off wandering in the dark. Shu was air and Tefnut was moisture and neither of them had special powers to let them see through the blackness. So, as children will, they got lost.

When Ra realized they were absent, he felt bereft. The difference between being alone in the vastness and being with his two children was the difference between sorrow and delight. He was lonely. And, worse, he grew anxious. There could be nothing out there to hurt the children, for, after all, there could be nothing out there period. What existed existed only because Ra had made it. Yet anxiety made this god itch all over until he wanted to scream and scratch his own skin off. He needed those children. He loved them.

At this time Ra had only one eye. He plucked it out from his forehead and sent his eye searching for Shu and Tefnut, for his darlings.

Then he settled down and waited for the eye to return. He waited and waited. While he waited, blind and cold, he curled in on himself and wondered what he would do if his eye didn't find the children. It might search in vain forever. But the children could come back on their own anyway— that was possible. But that was terrible, too, for their father wouldn't even be able to see them. Ra rolled in wretchedness.

And so Ra fashioned for himself a new eye, as he waited and waited some more.

Meanwhile the first eye of Ra, the original eye, lit up the world and flew across the firmament. It hugged the sands. It seeped into rock crevices. And now it soared across the waters, rising with each wave, falling as it crested. The old eye checked everywhere, everywhere and at last found the cowering cubs, who had grown all gangly and awkward, almost full size by now, and led them back to their father, dripping and skinny and needy.

Tefnut and her brother Shu coiled up in fear, lost without the warmth and light of their father Ra. This is how Ra's original eye found them—shivering.

RA (HELIOS)

RA (HELIOS)

Ra's tears of relief and love fell freely, bursting as they hit the earth and, thus, releasing human beings into the world. And a whole lot of trouble.

Ra gathered his children to his chest and felt whole again. These children were his very limbs, they were his own breath, his own fluids, they were everything. He broke himself on the joy of being reunited and he wept on his parts. With great huge sobs, he exhausted himself. And strange creatures—human beings—stepped delicately out of each teardrop, resplendent in their wet newness, gaping at the awe-inspiring wonder of creation. Innocent, yes. Yet with hungry hearts that made Ra's new eye blink, for he sensed those hungry human hearts would allow innocence to be consumed and vanish.

But the old eye of Ra, the original eye, was glad to see that humans were corruptible. That eye wanted Ra's creations to make trouble for him, for Ra had been disloyal—Ra had replaced the old eye with the new eye. The old eye smoldered in fury.

Ra was stupefied at the old eye's reaction. He understood nothing of jealousy, nothing of loyalty. Those emotions came from interacting, and he had never had to interact with anyone but Tefnut and Shu. Still, as his old eye hissed and spluttered, he understood the need for appeasement. And so he transformed his old eye into a snake, the very first snake ever, a cobra. And he picked it up and put it on the front of his forehead—the place of highest honor—and he called it his *iaret*. It worked! The iaret was proud to precede Ra wherever he went.

Everything was getting better and better.

But now something else was happening. Snakes slithered across Ra's feet. They slithered across Shu's and Tefnut's feet. Amazing: Creation had led to more creation. Shu and Tefnut considered the snakes and they knew, as though by instinct, that they could create, too. Air and moisture can dance together, after all. A mist, Shu and Tefnut tangoed over the unending sea, they dipped and twirled in graceful embrace, and Shu breathed into Tefnut until they gave birth to Geb and Nut.

The new generation lay there, tangled in a heated hug, so much so that they risked merging entirely.

Ra and his daughter Tefnut looked on with puzzled interest, but the god Shu knew better. Nothing could happen right if Geb and Nut didn't separate. Shu sensed that life wanted to crawl forth on the back of Geb and for that to happen, light needed to dance between Geb and Nut. So Shu did what a father had to do; he tore Geb and Nut asunder. He raised Nut up in his long strong arms to make an arch of sky, leaving Geb prostrate, the waiting earth, ready for whatever gifts might come from above and below.

But Ra didn't wait for anything; it wasn't in his nature. He looked at the bow Nut's body formed and all those words that filled his heart now spilled out of his mouth in a new form: stories. Ra became brilliant like Nut, brilliant with stories. He had to tell those stories, those

stories could make anything happen, anytime, anywhere.

Ra snuck behind the mountain Manu (which appeared even as he said the name) and climbed into his boat *Manjet* (again gaining solidity as it was named, yet somehow being as old as forever, millions upon millions of years old) and sailed across the sky as a glowing ball of fire that appeared to roll over Nut's thighs and buttocks and spine and neck. He landed in the far west horizon (since the directions now existed as he spoke them) and then journeyed back to Manu,

Shu lifted his daughter Nut; the drape of her body formed the sky. He left his son Geb lying at his feet; the expanse of Geb's body formed the earth.

Manjet carried Ra across the sky, as he changed from a morning babe to an evening sage. Imagine how strange it must have felt to experience a lifetime each day.

to his starting point, this time traveling through the underworld Duat in his second boat, *Mesektet.*

There was something exhilarating and renewing at the start of the journey across the sky and something tiring and withering at the end. A tantalizing mix. Ra had to repeat it; it was far too involving to experience only once. He allowed himself to be born again, coming out through Nut as though she were his mother rather than his granddaughter, reversing the order of things, confusing time by letting it circle back on itself. He rose as a baby. By midday, when the boat *Manjet* arrived at the first knob of Nut's spine, he was a man in the prime of life, a hero ready to tackle any problem and win. He set in the evening as an old man, tottering on a short stick, a flame fanning to a flicker of heat and finally a memory of warmth. What a journey.

RA (HELIOS)

What a thrill. He had to repeat it forever.

And so a new order was formed. The sun god Ra defined the fundamental rhythm of life. But disorder could never disappear now; life entails it. And Ra's words ensured it.

Pay attention, all.
Behold my majesty.
I am the Lord of Radiance.
I am the father of all, the lover of strength, the giant of victory.
So now, let us conquer.

Conquer? What could that mean? Who was there to conquer? Where was the disorder, the discord, that would require vanquishing? Ra couldn't see it yet. But he knew beyond a doubt it was coming.

RA (HELIOS)

THE GREAT PESEDJET
A Hierarchy of Gods

The sun god Ra created himself, then his children: the air god Shu and the moisture goddess Tefnut. They created their children: the earth god Geb and the sky goddess Nut. Now the ball was rolling; Geb, in all his lush splendor with plants growing from him, and Nut, in all her quiet splendor with winds caressing her, did their part, singly and together. Soon there were five children in the next generation: the goddess Nebet Hut and her husband-brother god Set, the goddess Aset and her husband-brother god Usir, and the god Heru Wer. Ra was progenitor to nine more deities now, the Great Pesedjet. *(See illustration left)*

Ra had been pleased at the triad that he and Shu and Tefnut formed. But now, all these progeny totaled nine, and nine was better. Nine was three squared. A nine-pointed star could be formed by superimposing three identical equilateral triangles, so that each was rotated precisely 40 degrees over from the next lower one. A magic square could be formed by making a matrix of nine cells within a square, each one filled with a distinct numeral from 1 to 9, where the numbers in each row, the numbers in each column, and the numbers in each of the two diagonals added up to the same total. The geometric and algebraic games one could play with nine were a delight. They were a promise of an extraordinary future. And the best thing about the Great Pesedjet was that Ra's

Hut Heru was grace itself, enriching the world with the joys of the senses. She was dance and music, inextricably intertwined, and decoratively beautiful, night and day.

great-grandson Heru Wer was really just the embodiment of Ra himself at midday. So Ra could count himself as part of this miraculous nine. Ra was pleased beyond measure.

That pleasure excited Ra into an even more heated frenzy of creativity that needed to live up to the cleverness of the number nine. The molten flow that had emerged from the watery Nun with Ra's first words still sizzled. It now inspired Ra. With flame coming from his pointing finger he made the basic elements to build all things. He started with iron and blew it over this rapidly forming ball of a world. It glittered golden. A royal satisfaction enveloped Ra; this was fated to be his color, the rightful color of the father of everything and everyone.

But the world needed more colors. Another jab of Ra's fire fingertip scattered red lithium to the winds. Next calcium burned bright orange. Then sodium flamed yellow, copper sparkled green, selenium glowed blue,

THE GREAT PESEDJET

cesium flashed indigo, potassium gave violet luster.

The luminosity of colors seduced Ra's new eye to step forward as a goddess, and she called herself Hut Heru. She danced over the earth, on which the iron had now cooled into a crust, and laughed, filling the cosmos with music. The twirling of her skirts swished the remaining gassy colors high. When the sun god Ra shone his light through the moisture goddess Tefnut, a rainbow arched across the world, echoing the arched body of Nut, the daughter of Tefnut and Shu.

Hut Heru didn't always dance, though. She loved night. She lay back in those hours and gazed upward into nothingness. So she wanted calming colors for those quiet times. Ra knew this, of course, for Hut Heru was his very eye. With a scorching finger, he made the silver of aluminum. From it the stars and moon formed, and Hut Heru was glad and grateful.

Now there were nine colors. Nine again. Luscious nine.

Ra shrugged and a cloud of insects filled the air in all imaginable colors. He loved scarabs best. They rolled dung into balls and laid their eggs inside, so the little balls emitted heat as the dung decayed. Later, when the eggs hatched, it seemed like spontaneous generation—like the self-generation of the royal Ra. What charming creatures! Ra took to assuming scarab form and calling himself Ra-Khepra in the morning, when he was just a babe pushing the sun up into the sky. From then on the scarab was sacred before all other creatures.

But the insects swarmed, far too many, plaguing the Pesedjet of deities. So the tongue of Ra stepped forward, as the god Tehuti, and with ever-powerful words he created birds to eat them. Clever Ra was wiser now about the ways of life, so he didn't stop there; he made Tehuti speak again, and now some birds preyed upon others, to keep the populations of both insects and birds under control. The master predator and most intelligent was the falcon, and so Ra declared it his bird. Ra often assumed the head of a falcon, particularly in midday at the sun's zenith. In that form he called himself Ra-Herakhty.

The falcons were such skillful hunters, they would soon have eaten up all the smaller birds except for the fact that

There was a whole world to fill, and Ra did it all. Just a blink, a shrug, a chin flick, and wings flapped, feet scurried, bodies wriggled.

they had the snakes to prey upon, as well. Perfect.

And those snakes—good glory, what killers the cobras were! Their tongues picked up the faintest smells and the pits behind their nostrils were so sensitive to heat that they could hunt even at night. Ra had been brilliant to add the sacred iaret to his headdress.

Through words, Ra created little creatures of land and sea and air. Then medium-size ones. Then enormous ones. He created plants and mushrooms. He created rocks and metals and gases. And it was all so painfully beautiful.

Ra gazed at the world through his new eye Hut Heru, wearing his sacred iaret, and the complexity impressed him—the deities, the plants, the beasts, the humans. But somehow those humans kept worrying him. They were cunning in a different way from the beasts. Ra had the terrible sense that he had known those humans would bring trouble, that he had willfully played his part. This was how it had to be. And just as strongly he felt all creation was teetering, close to going out of control.

SET (SETH)
Envious God

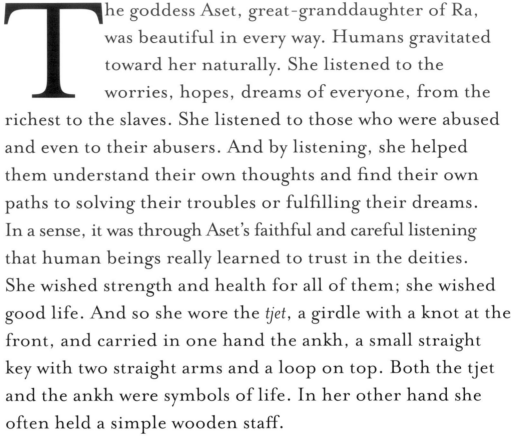

The goddess Aset, great-granddaughter of Ra, was beautiful in every way. Humans gravitated toward her naturally. She listened to the worries, hopes, dreams of everyone, from the richest to the slaves. She listened to those who were abused and even to their abusers. And by listening, she helped them understand their own thoughts and find their own paths to solving their troubles or fulfilling their dreams. In a sense, it was through Aset's faithful and careful listening that human beings really learned to trust in the deities. She wished strength and health for all of them; she wished good life. And so she wore the *tjet*, a girdle with a knot at the front, and carried in one hand the ankh, a small straight key with two straight arms and a loop on top. Both the tjet and the ankh were symbols of life. In her other hand she often held a simple wooden staff.

That wooden staff was useful when she walked with her brother-husband Usir in the fields. Usir loved to wander among the animals, particularly the animals that humans quickly gathered around them. And even more particularly those fat woolly sheep with the wide-set eyes that made that little *baaa baaa* noise Aset found so pleasing. In fact, Usir was so fond of sheep, he wore ram horns on his crown. He was a benevolent god, bringing robustness to the sheep and fertility to the land. He taught humans to plow and he gave them laws to live by, rising to become king of Lower Egypt and then, so popular was he, king of all Egypt. And so it was impossible for this benevolent god not to love his ever-so-benevolent wife Aset. He adored her. They were meant for each other.

Their brother god Set watched them gaze at each other, this Aset and this Usir, eavesdropping on their fond murmurings. He could smell how they changed when they approached each other. Usir grew musky, like a young ram; his muscles rippled under his skin. Aset became as fragrant as those water flowers she picked so often, those blue lotuses. She grew intoxicating, as though her very essence was lotus oil.

Set had a sister-wife of his own—what was her name? Ah, yes, Nebet Hut. But Set couldn't think about her. He couldn't even look at her. He looked instead at Aset.

THE LOTUS: God Scent

Ancient Egypt had both white and blue lotuses, and from both an oil can be extracted that is pungently sweet to smell. People used the flowers as decoration and women used the essence of the lotus as perfume. Egyptian perfumes have been famous from ancient times through modern times. But the blue lotus also has a high plant nutrient content, so this flower may have been used by the ancients in medicines for its healing properties.

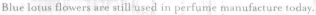

Blue lotus flowers are still used in perfume manufacture today.

All that love heaped on his brother galled Set. Alas, he couldn't think of anything else, he couldn't enjoy ordinary things, he couldn't love anyone.

And he looked at Usir. He looked until his eyes burned as dry as the desert he prowled.

Then the strands of envy twisted even tighter around Set's innards, for his brother Usir fawned over Set's son Inpu. Set's teeth went grimy with disgust. And Inpu, the ingrate, he responded to this attention, caring for his uncle Usir too much—he even seemed to take after him. Intolerable—it was Set the boy should love like that! So Set was glad when the boy left home to go work in

SET (SETH)

the underworld Duat. Who needed such a son around?

But still Set had to watch Aset's face as she gazed at Usir. And now he looked around and noticed how humans adored this sister and this brother that they had chosen as their queen and king, and his top lip curled. There were so many humans by now—they just kept multiplying. And that meant Set's brother Usir was king of far too much, and was loved by far too many.

Sometimes a brother doesn't need a reason to be spiteful toward another brother. Set was almost sure he would have hated Usir no matter what, regardless of how Aset loved him, regardless of how his own son Inpu admired him. But the way all those people loved Usir—well, that went beyond the pale. King of Egypt! Bah! Set's insides swirled like the very strongest of tempests, with lightning and thunder and shrieking winds— and in this stormy state he vowed to himself to crush Usir.

Set held a banquet. He arranged cones of scented fat in a large circle and set them ablaze to keep away pesky mosquitoes. He gave the goddesses lotus flower necklaces—knowing, of course, that this would endear him to Aset. He filled a basin with sparkling clean water for everyone to wash their hands in. Then he served them bread and great quantities of beer. As they were lolling around, satiated, he pulled a cloth away to reveal a beautiful box.

Usir ran his hand appreciatively along the intricate carvings. "Where did you get this, brother?"

Usir slid happily into the majestic cedar box. It felt like the most comfortable of beds. How cold must Set's heart have been, planning the doom ahead.

The combination of gold gilt, the color so dear to the great god Ra, and deep blue paint, the color so dear to his beloved wife Aset, made the box nearly irresistible to the unsuspecting Usir.

"It's superb, isn't it?" Set leaned in toward Usir with a brotherly intimacy. "Tell you what. Whoever fits perfectly in this box, well, that's the rightful owner of it. I will regale that person with this fine box."

Each guest took a turn at lying in the box. But each was too short or too long or too fat or too thin. In contrast, Usir fit perfectly. Naturally. For Set had taken all the relevant measures

SET (SETH)

of his brother as he slept, and had the box built just so.

The instant Usir lay inside, Set and his helpers rushed forward, closed the lid, and sealed it. Set lifted the box over his head and flung it with all his might into the raging Nile River. And for the first time in so long he couldn't remember, Set felt triumph. He was rid of Usir, rid of the scourge of his life. At last, he could be all he wanted to be; he stood in no one's shadow.

Such is the brutality unchecked envy can wreak.

But good has its own way of responding—and both Aset and Usir were deeply good. This story was far from its end.

ASET (ISIS)
Devoted Wife and Mother

The god Set was so envious of his brother Usir that he committed a dastardly act. He nailed Usir into a box and threw it into the Nile River.

"Ahiii," screamed Aset. She ran along the shore, arms outstretched futilely. She must catch up, she must pull the box to safety. She imagined her husband trapped inside, panicked. She ran.

But the current raced north, carrying her husband inexorably toward the sea. And the wind blew south, impeding Aset's every step. She ran hard, seeing the white-foamed swirl of the swift and wild river. She ran harder, hearing nothing but the shriek of the wind rasping her ears raw. The box was already out of sight! Aset had to run yet faster. That was her husband—the love of her life!

Aset ran all that day, all that night, all the next day. Her feet bled. Her legs ached. When she arrived at the seashore, she raced back and forth, calling out over the green and blue and purple waters, calling, calling. She rent her hair. She grabbed a clamshell and shaved off her eyebrows. She beat her chest.

The world spun around this goddess, this woman in love, bereft and alone, who had no choice but to prostrate herself on the beach and wait for the dizziness to pass and hope against hope that her husband had managed to get out of the box before he suffocated.

Our Alphabet's History

A tablet showing the Phoenician alphabet

The Kenaani's land became known as Phoenicia. It spread between the River Jordan and the Mediterranean Sea. The people were known for sea trading and purple dye made from murex snails. But we know them most for their *abjad,* a writing system with letters that represented consonant sounds. The Greeks borrowed this abjad and added letters for vowels. The Etruscans then borrowed it, then the Romans, each making changes—hence our alphabet.

Meanwhile the box that held Usir had washed out to the middle of the vast Mediterranean Sea and floated in that *wadj wer*—that great green—aimlessly, a rudderless, sail-less skiff, until the currents eventually carried it toward shore again. But not back to the mouth of the Nile where miserable Aset lay crying, no. The box settled far to the east, near the city of Kubna in the land of the Kenaani.

The coast there was thick with strong reeds that reached out. Like tentacles, they slipped around and over and under each other and pulled the box in, wrapping themselves about it over and over, caressingly. Somehow one reed pushed against another so insistently that the two reeds merged, and then another merged with them, and soon the mass of reeds was a single shrub engulfing the box. And then the shrub grew.

This sort of magic doesn't happen every day—and magic it surely was. For inside that box lay the corpse of the god Usir, who had known how to bring fertility to the earth, who could make anything grow. So perhaps that very power had transferred from the god to the box as he gave his last breath. Who can know such a thing? Yet that shrub grew faster than any shrub had ever grown before, and became a massive cedar tree, 130 feet tall, studded with cones. Hoopoe birds came in droves to give themselves sand baths under the tree and to nest among its silver-green needle-like leaves.

The mighty cedar could be seen from afar, but it could be smelled even before it was seen, for it gave off a spicy, alluring aroma. Soon the king himself noticed the tree, and he called his queen to his side to inhale its essence. She swooned at the cedar perfume. After all, she was late in her pregnancy and she was given to swooning.

There was no question about it: The tree was majestic, it must grace the king's palace. It took a troop of workers to cut through the base and haul the tree to the palace, where it became a beautiful column that all could admire. And they did. The column made them feel a certain peace; it offered a sense of assurance that all would be well with the world. It was almost godly in that way. Yet still, no one guessed that inside the trunk nestled the box that held Usir.

The gigantic cedar that held Usir's trunk was one of many colossal trees in that land. They could live thousands of years. But this tree was doomed.

ASET (ISIS)

Grief-stricken Aset somehow sensed the birds knew best. She followed their calls to the palace of Kubna, where her husband Usir was hidden within the cedar column.

Back on the shore of Egypt, the goddess Aset lay desperate. Moons had passed and still she remained immobile. But now she was woken from her grief-stricken stupor by the insistent calls *bu bu bu*, and again *bu bu bu*, all around her *bu bu bu*. She sat up, agog at the flock of hoopoes with their colorful crests, strutting in profusion. These were the birds who had nested in the cedar the king had cut down; they were mourning its loss. They had flown all this way searching for a substitute tree when they'd spotted Aset, and instinctively they were drawn to her, instinctively they understood her grief matched theirs.

The birds called *bu bu bu* and Aset stood. *Bu bu bu*. The birds took to the air and circled above her. Aset followed, and the procession moved east, a wavering line along the sands, a spiraling in the heavens.

Aset sensed an urgency in the birds and hope swelled her heart. These birds were leading her to Usir. What else could this mean? With each day her hopes grew till her heart was ready to shred.

There, at long last, was the splendid palace of Kubna. Aset wandered, sure the box would be just past that wall, just 'round that corner, just under that eave. But the box was nowhere!

Without warning, without preamble, reason finally coated Aset's tongue with a bitter salt: Usir was dead. Whether she found the box or not, he was dead. It was almost as though he was nearby, with his spirit telling her that, forcing her to understand.

Aset found a large, smooth, warm rock in the courtyard. She sat and wept. But these were tears of acceptance and exhaustion. It was over. At last.

So she thought.

But inside the Kubna palace the royal handmaidens whispered. A morose stranger sat in the courtyard. She was thin as a wind-whipped pine, but still one could see a beauty in those cheekbones, that long neck, those cupped hands. The royal handmaidens peeked out at her, wary at first, but then, gradually, worried for her. Grief weighed on the stranger so heavily, it hurt them to watch. This woman was broken. They approached on quiet feet.

Aset turned and saw their frightened faces and her wounded heart opened. After all, her grief was due to no fault of theirs. She smiled through tears and patted the empty spot on the rock beside her. These handmaidens were hardly older than girls, innocent and fresh. She plaited their hair and exhaled perfume onto their golden skin, and when they asked what had happened to her, she talked sweetly of nothing. Deities knew that humans weren't good at discussions about death.

The afternoon passed and one by one the maidens left. Aset folded one hand inside the other and sat. She wasn't waiting. There was nothing to wait for. She was resting.

Soon those maidens reappeared and took Aset by both hands and led her to their queen, recommending her sincerely.

The queen paused, a finger pressed to her cheek. "You're not like what the girls said. Not at all."

Aset didn't speak. She wasn't even sure why she was still standing there. She might as well leave.

"You're older than my usual handmaidens. But I sense your true value."

Aset jerked to attention. She looked closely at this queen now, at the tired eyes, the flushed cheeks. Did she really know she was in the presence of a goddess?

ASET (ISIS)

"I sense the good in you. You can help me in the way I most need help." The queen bid Aset to follow her into another chamber—an infant's chamber. The queen picked up her newborn son and placed him in Aset's arms. "You're his new nursemaid."

Beautiful child! Tiny hands with slender fingers and nearly transparent nails, tiny feet with toes that curled at a touch. A mouth that rounded when Aset rounded hers. Eyes that blinked when Aset blinked hers. A round head that gave off the scent of honey, with hair softer than down. What a perfect thing was a baby. Oh, how Aset wished that she and Usir had had children, for then she could go on loving him through the babe.

But for now it was enough to love this queen's baby, this perfect prince. Aset bathed him and sang to him and held him close. She nuzzled his ear. She adored him.

And soon the tiny prince adored Aset.

Bereaved Aset, the woman who thought she would never bear a child now that she was a widow, received the precious prince into her loving arms.

The swallow that was Aset flew above the flames that engulfed her sweet prince. This was to be magic, to render the boy immune from death. Alas, the queen thwarted all.

ASET (ISIS)

Then one day, as she leaned against a wide pillar she had taken a liking to, it occurred to Aset that the prince would grow old and die. He would leave her, just as Usir had. She couldn't go through that pain again.

She had to prevent it. She would confer immortality upon the babe. She could do that! All it took was the right spell and the purification of fire.

Aset gathered cedar brush—for there was much lying near the pillar—and set it aflame. She placed the baby in the fire. He screamed. It was all she could do to keep herself from snatching him back. Yet she mustn't—she mustn't. She transformed herself into a swallow, flying round the huge pillar. The child shrieked. But it wouldn't be long now, the spell was nearly complete, Aset had to keep circling that pillar.

The queen rushed in and pulled the blistered baby from the embers. Aset's yowl pierced the cosmos. The queen had ruined everything. Instantly, Aset became herself again and revealed that she was a goddess. She demanded that the pillar be split open and that a massive fire be built so she could make the prince immortal.

When the workers split the pillar, the box with Usir fell out. It was still nailed shut, sealed off from air. Aset's cry of grief nearly strangled her.

And it did strangle the baby prince. He died in his mother's arms. Tragedy upon tragedy.

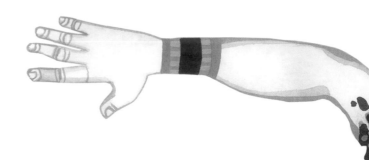

Aset put the coffin in a boat and brought it back to Egypt. She would bury her husband as soon as they arrived home. Yet once they were on Egyptian soil, the desire seized her to open the coffin for one last embrace. Alas, piteous sight. Aset wept on the wasted body of Usir. She closed the coffin and hid it in a swamp while she prepared herself for the rituals of burial.

But during these months Set had learned to transform himself into a fabulous beast, the terror of the desert, with the belly and back of a wolf, a long snout that could pick up any odor, square ears that could detect any sound, and a bent tail that warned others off. Fearsome and vicious, he hunted in that form by night. And that very night Set, when he was out hunting, came across the coffin.

He opened it and ripped Usir's body into 14 pieces. He threw the scrappy lumps of his brother as far as he could, across the face of Egypt. This way Aset could never give him a proper burial; Usir could never be whole in the ever-after. Set had made mayhem of Aset's and Usir's lives.

Monstrous with envy, Set shredded his brother Usir's corpse, scattering the pieces. This way he thought he'd steal Usir's peace in the afterlife, just as he'd stolen it in this life.

ASET (ISIS)

In victory, he yowled so loud the earth shook.

Yet still the story is not at its end, for good must prevail—or we would all be strangers to hope.

Aset wept. She sobbed.

Set's sister-wife Nebet Hut felt splintered. No one could watch the misery of Aset and not be touched. But it was Nebet Hut's husband who had caused this misery. It was Set—that wild god Set. Didn't a wife owe loyalty to her husband, even if he was wild? Nebet Hut chewed her knuckles. Her eyes grew glassy.

Aset's tears fell in the Nile River till it overflowed and flooded the lands. And still she cried.

Nebet Hut shook her head. There were all kinds of loyalty. Aset was her sister, and Usir was her brother, after all. And there was also a touchy and secret matter concerning Nebet Hut's son Inpu—something that involved Usir and that made Nebet Hut feel she owed Aset.

And so she went to Aset and helped her gather the parts of Usir. They watched for circling birds of prey—a clue every time—and ran from one grisly site to another, until they had collected 13 pieces. But the fourteenth, where was it?

"Lossst," hissed a passing serpent. "Lossst in a marsh monsssster."

In grief, Aset rolled in the mud.

An ibis waded past making his quiet *grrrr,* the throaty noise of breeding. And Aset knew this was the god Tehuti, the tongue of

Aset and Usir had one last night together as man and wife before he had to leave her forever. They used it wisely to seal their love in a child.

the god Ra, come to give advice. So she let out a low, guttural wail, mimicking Tehuti's, and the pieces of Usir assembled themselves, and Aset fashioned the missing part out of wax and clay, so Usir was whole, and she kissed him into consciousness.

Usir looked at her with a vacant, slack face, but Aset kept kissing him and soon both were lost in the sweet delight of matrimony.

When Aset woke in the morning, she reached for her love. Alas! Usir was gone. She had known he had to leave, it was inevitable. The magic wail Tehuti had taught Aset, the wail that brought Usir to life again, was not strong enough to maintain that life. Husband and wife were together only one night. Blessed and wondrous night, unique in its shattering beauty. But gone. Done.

Yet Aset was not alone: She was with child. She'd sensed this even the night before—it was an instant understanding. No one aboveground knew, however, and it was essential that no one find out, for the world had turned hostile. Usir was now safe in the underworld Duat. But Aset was still above, still walking the hot sands of Egypt, still haunted by her murderous brother Set. Set had usurped the lands formerly ruled by Usir; he sat on his brother's throne, shameless. Aset's bones would have clacked if her flesh didn't clothe them. No evil was beyond the monster Set. He must not find out about the child within Aset.

So Aset took off her tjet, the girdle with the filigreed buckle and the intricate knot, and let her gowns flow loose. She bent forward, leaning over her staff, as though her back ached. No one saw the bulges in her belly when the child

Aset knew the monster Set would be a danger to her and Usir's child. So she hid the babe within by walking stooped in flowing gowns.

ASET (ISIS)

inside thrashed about. Sometimes Aset couldn't hold in the smiles those kicks brought. But if anyone asked what made her happy, she recounted the antics of the human children that she was so fond of visiting. Indeed, human women watched how Aset played with their children and they called her the goddess of fertility. They asked her help on matters of family life. They asked how to maintain domestic tranquillity, questions that flustered Aset, because she was the last one to understand that. Look what her brother had done to her husband, just look if you dared. A shiver shot up her spine.

But she was defiant. Though she was not beside Usir physically, she was beside him in thoughts. The last night they were together, he had said she was like the welcome north wind on the hottest days. He called her the sweet wind that refreshes, and that new name now lived around her as an aura. It brushed her cheek so softly that she couldn't help but turn her face toward it, like a babe turns to meet the source of food. She felt more enlivened with each day. Yes, she could manage in this life—yes, this was good.

And it could get better. Aset learned that Usir had taken a ruling role in the underworld. She decided to help him in this task. Why not? She couldn't abide down in Duat—for she was alive. And she couldn't be a true wife to Usir—for he was dead. But she could visit and stand behind him as he judged the dead. She could blow him kisses, she could be truly the sweet wind that refreshes. Why not? Oh, why not? Who could begrudge her this small concession?

What a joy it was the first time to stand before Usir again in Duat. His eyes were pools of devotion, salty sweet and buoyant—a place to swim, not drown. Then Usir reached out his large hand—that hand that had caressed Aset, whose memory she indulged in each night—and laid it heavily on Aset's belly and felt the life within, and Aset cried out. Just one cry of loss. For she had to smile, as well. She could manage in this life. Now that she could see Usir again, she could really manage.

Finally, the labor pains started. Aset fled to that same swamp in the delta where she'd hidden Usir's coffin nine months earlier. There the child was born, and Aset named him Heru after his uncle Heru Wer. Since Ra and Heru Wer spent much time together, Aset hoped Ra would take a special interest in Heru Sa Aset—Heru son of Aset—and might even protect him. But she didn't count on it. Up aboveground, Aset counted on no one but herself.

She raised her son in secret.

But she knew it would take more than determination and cleverness to keep Heru Sa Aset safe. It would take magic. A spasm racked her—for she had failed so badly in the magic she'd tried to wield to make the little prince of Kubna immortal. Still, Aset shouldn't be so scared. After all, she had brought Usir back to life that one beautiful

night—that was magic. The key was not in transformations and fires, but in the power of words. How obvious. The god Ra had created everything from words. Aset should have recognized that was the right route from the start. Words were the charm.

And so Aset decided to cultivate the magic of words. She would succeed this time.

How? How could she learn?

And there they were: humans. They swarmed like bees. They were both weak and foolish, so they were continually getting sick and injured. They presented the perfect opportunity for a budding magician to practice on.

Aset cured a cold. Simple enough. She made firm a broken bone. Ha! She calmed a head gone crazy from fear and banished a growth that would have eventually sucked life away. Wahoo! Whatever the ailment, Aset found within herself the words to heal it. She was good at this, and she kept getting better. She had

Heru Sa Aset was born among lotus blossoms, just as his father Usir died there. That swamp became his home for years— his special place, safe from Set.

ASET (ISIS)

to get perfect—nothing less could protect against Set.

One day a lethal scorpion stung Heru Sa Aset, Aset's treasured child. She had never tried to cure a god before. But instantly, without prompt, she named the scorpion. That's all it took. A name, and with it Aset gained power over the scorpion and his poison. The god-boy revived in one breath.

Yes! Aset was at the top of her prowess.

And still fear gnawed at her. Set was the prince of darkness, the blight of the cosmos. Aset had to be the most powerful magician ever. So Aset resolved to take a terrible chance.

The sun god Ra had grown old, and stumbly in his walk. He drooled, as old men do.

Aset followed him, quiet as a shadow. She scooped up that drool and mixed it with dirt and rolled out a snake that she filled with a poison only she knew the antidote to.

In the morning, when Ra went to make his journey across the sky, the snake struck so fast Ra never saw it. The god groaned and threw himself around. The pain was terrible and terrifying. His leg swelled double. His arms tingled. His whole body tingled. He screamed.

Geb and Nut and Tefnut and Shu came rushing.

"What happened?"

"I don't know. Heal me. Use magic."

"Tehuti! I'll fetch Tehuti."

"Not just Tehuti. Find Aset. She's the best magician."

But Aset was already there. She'd been there all along, of course, hiding. She stepped past the others now and made a show of examining Ra carefully. Her hands trembled from the deceit. But she was a mother—whatever else she was, she was a mother with a son to protect. She proclaimed, "A snakebite."

"Ack! The very worst!" Ra fell to the ground and panted. "Heal me!"

"I will." Aset turned to the others. "Stand back. We need room for the magic to work." When the others were out of hearing range, Aset put her lips to Ra's ear. "I'll cure you. But first, tell me your secret name."

Every deity had a secret name. If Aset knew Ra's, she could have Ra's powers. She would become as powerful as him. She could protect her son Heru Sa Aset.

Ra rolled his head from side to side. No god had yet revealed that secret to any other. But the serpent's toxins were fierce. Already his vision blurred. The rosy dawn turned gray. He was dizzy and nauseated.

Snakebites were one of the greatest dangers in ancient Egypt, not just to humans and animals, but also to gods. Even Ra was helpless against the cobra's venom.

ASET (ISIS)

"I am the creator of the cosmos," he choked out, "the ripener of crops. I wear a solar disk on my head and I bring heat."

"Those aren't names."

"At dawn I am Ra-Khepra, the scarab." Ra breathed with difficulty. "At noon I am Ra-Herakhty, the falcon." His throat was closing. "At night I am—"

"No!" Aset's own eyes blurred with tears. This old man was her great-grandfather and she was letting him decay, moment by moment. She had caused this. If he remained stubborn, his blood would stain her hands for eternity. Yet she wouldn't

ASET (ISIS)

say the magic words—she wouldn't abandon her son. "Everyone knows these names, great Ra. I need your secret name."

"Help me, Aset."

Her heart broke. But she controlled her tongue; those magic words must not escape. "Your secret name. Your essence. Don't fail me. Please. Nothing less will do."

And so Ra whispered to Aset with what would have been his last breath, and she cured him in the nick of time.

From then on, Ra ruled only in the heavens, and Aset ruled on earth, and, of course, her husband Usir ruled below. Everyone thought this was Aset's grand plan; she wanted supreme power. They didn't know about her son. They didn't know her goal was simply to protect him.

But that's exactly what she did, until he was a young man, strong and clear-eyed and ready. Then she told the other deities that Heru Sa Aset was here, his father's son, and the rightful heir to his father's throne. That's when Heru Sa Aset's struggles began.

Aset made the snake whose bite only she could cure. A treacherous thing for a great-granddaughter to do. But she was a mother first; she had a son to protect.

ASET (ISIS)

USIR (OSIRIS)
God of the Afterlife

Usir's head spun. How had he arrived here? But the love of his life was kissing him and right now that's all that mattered.

The couple plucked clusters from the tops of papyrus and made a feathery bed to share. Woman of the lotus, man of the papyrus—union of Upper and Lower Egypt. Rare and tender night.

It was a moment of perfect happiness. They knew within Aset's womb a son grew.

It was a moment of utter sadness. They knew this was their last time as wife and husband; once death comes, even to a god, life on earth is past.

Usir woke at dawn, green as papyrus, kissed his sleeping sister-wife goodbye, and walked into the waters, still uncomprehending, aware only that this was preordained. He must leave this land, this wife, this life.

When had the Nile become so wide? Then he tasted the salt of sorrow . . . his wife's tears. In a vision of memory that wasn't his, Usir saw Aset wandering. Her raw feet, hoarse throat, ragged heart. He raged at such sadness. He could do nothing to salve past wounds. But he would honor the enduring grief. Yes, he would make the river flood yearly. When the waters retreated, they would leave behind silt to enrich the land so plants would find purchase. The land would resurrect, to match

The Nile: Flooding

The Nile River flooded annually until a dam was built at Aswan (completed in 1970). Flooding brought nutritious silt to the riverbanks, and made a thin ribbon of productive soil in the middle of a country that otherwise was m[...] sand and clay. Villagers paid taxes to the central government based on how high the river flooded in their area, where the flood height was measured in wells beside the temple of the local gods.

The Nile River surrounded by lush greenery

Usir's resurrection. Sheep would [...] a *baaa*, bleating praise to Usir's spirit. Usir laughe[...] good would come of his death: an abundant ha[...]h year. A fitting homage to the tragedy of Aset and [...]

Usir swam with the Nile fish and it f[...]l, as though water was home. The sheath that covered him [...] not scales, but it was green and hope-studded. The worl[...] with the current.

The current, the flow, the bobbing [...]ating.

In a blink all changed. More dark r[...]s, but these threatened his sanity, for these were h[...]

He was alive in that beautifully carved box, in bla[...] only the clean smell of cedar. As he pushed and shouted and strug[...] st the lid, that mild smell was overpowered by the acrid odor of his sou[...] he stench of mortal fear: There was little air in this tomb. His mouth a[...] in and then insides

Usir saw that the river had risen because his wife had wept so hard for loss of him. How strange, to immerse himself in Aset's tears even as he left her.

USIR (OSIRIS)

dried. He was cold. Lifeless. A miserable wretch, for he would have no funeral, no tomb for his wife to honor. Eternally alone.

Then everything changed. He was dead still, sealed in his coffin still — *knew Aset was close. She carried him home. She would right this most wrong. But then Set came and shredded him. Usir's parts would have if they could: Never whole, never whole.*

Until Aset made him whole. How she had done i didn't know. But he knew their love had transform he became the sweet wind that refreshes. True love c nat.

Usir hadn't realized that Set despised him un moment before that lid fell, when he saw Set's ed with envy, jealousy, naked need.

Could Set have discovered Usir's interlude wi Nebet Hut? It was a simple mistake, the sisters looked et Hut was the silent shade cast by her sister—a faint re it was only once. Such a high price to pay for an acci

Well, the price was now paid in full.

Usir's fresh green skin sloughed away in a poignant kiss goodbye. He grew black skin, dark as what lay beneath the earth. He swam to the underworld Duat where his nephew Inpu oversaw the dead. But Inpu yielded his supremacy there to Usir, a gesture of loyalty and love that touched Usir's heart.

Usir vowed to rule with mercy, for no one knew better than Usir how awful would be a world without mercy.

Goddess of Service

NEBET HUT (NEPHTHYS)
Goddess of Service

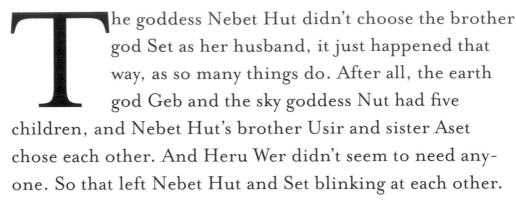

The goddess Nebet Hut didn't choose the brother god Set as her husband, it just happened that way, as so many things do. After all, the earth god Geb and the sky goddess Nut had five children, and Nebet Hut's brother Usir and sister Aset chose each other. And Heru Wer didn't seem to need anyone. So that left Nebet Hut and Set blinking at each other.

It didn't really surprise her, then, that Set showed no interest in her. It surprised her even less when Set's wandering eye fixed on her graceful sister Aset. (That was an irony Nebet Hut could have laughed at if it hadn't made her want to die.) And it felt nearly inevitable when Set remarked on how Usir and Aset's love of her own son Inpu revolted him.

Inpu wasn't really Set's son. This was a secret; not even Inpu knew. Nebet Hut had longed for a child. Pining had thinned and silvered her like the moon. Her hair had become wispy as strips of mummy cloth. So she'd romanced the sun god Ra. And she'd walked past her brother Usir in a place she knew he expected to find his wife Aset. Hence, Inpu. Whether Inpu's father was Ra or Usir, Nebet Hut couldn't say, but it was not Set.

This wasn't as dastardly as it might appear. Set didn't want a child with Nebet Hut, you see. He wanted Nebet Hut to interact with him as little as possible. He made that much obvious. So going to the sun god Ra was reasonable—fair.

And tricking Usir, well, what did that matter? Aset never knew, after all. Nebet Hut was good—she was: really—this was not her fault, hardly even her doing.

But she had to drug Set and lie with him, so he wouldn't realize Nebet Hut had strayed. A goddess did what a goddess had to do.

Nebet Hut believed this was why Set's lips curled at the boy. Set must have intuited that the child was not his. Perhaps he even saw something of Usir in him. That must have been part of Set's displeasure. A touch of jealousy? At some level, Set must have loved Nebet Hut to be stung with jealousy, no?

Nebet Hut realized this might be wishful thinking. She didn't know why, but she still clung to the illusion of her marriage to Set. She wished he'd want a child with her someday. So when Set killed their brother Usir, Nebet Hut was conflicted over whether to help poor Aset, her sister, or side

Desert Animals

Nebet Hut gains night vision and learns to breathe arid desert heat. In fact, many desert animals are nocturnal, taking advantage of the cold nights. Diurnal ones developed other ways to endure the heat. The "sandfish" skink dives into sand to cooler depths and "swims" there. Camels (whose ancestors evolved in North America, then thrived in Asia before spreading to Africa) control body heat to prevent sweating and reduce urination, allowing them to hold on to needed fluids.

Camels in the Egyptian desert ready to carry passengers on their backs with her brother-husband Set. But then she did what was right. What else can anyone do, no?

Aset repaid her in the dearest way: She enlisted Nebet Hut's help in the secret raising of Heru Sa Aset, Aset's son. She let Nebet Hut suckle Heru Sa Aset beside Inpu. In a sense the boy was as much Nebet Hut's as he was Aset's.

So much of Nebet Hut's life was spent loving children in secret. It had an effect. She felt most free at night, for the dark hid her as she kissed the boys and patted their heads in sleep. She learned to see by moonlight as easily as others saw by sunlight. If someone asked and if that someone was lucky, Nebet Hut would teach the arts of negotiating the night.

Sad Nebet Hut was unloved by her husband, but she found comfort in loving and being loved by her own son Inpu and by her sister's babe, the dear Heru Sa Aset.

NEBET HUT (NEPHTHYS)

She took to haunting perilous places others avoided. At first the edges of the desert, then far onto the scorching red sands, deep into the territory Set roamed. She learned to breathe the incredible heat in the heart of an arid wilderness, and expel fire from her mouth. She became formidable without trying. Humans asked her to incinerate their enemies, and she did. Why not? Why not protect Egypt? She'd follow these battles with lavish beer parties, for she had become a master brewer somehow.

Somehow, somehow. Everything happened to Nebet Hut somehow—in some way beyond her control—in some way that controlled her.

People loved her. And, as people will, they attributed powers to her. They called on her to assist in childbirth—Nebet Hut, whose own pains of childbirth had been riddled with guilt, helped women have joyful childbirth. People had faith in her as a healer. So Nebet Hut salved this wound, calmed those tremors, eased these aches.

She came to be goddess of the household, which felt fateful, since her name originally meant "mistress of the house." Funny how the world seemed to do what was intended from the start. She took to carrying a basket on her head, full of the necessities of daily life, food and swaddling clothes and ropes for making fishnet and rocks for grinding grain. She served. Yes, she served as best she could.

Young Warrior God and King

HERU SA ASET (HORUS THE YOUNGER)
Young Warrior God and King

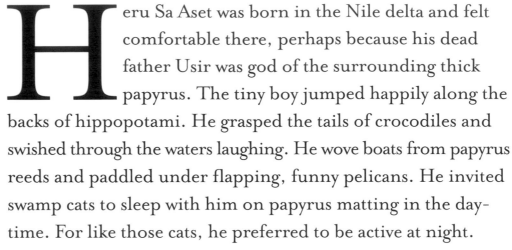

Heru Sa Aset was born in the Nile delta and felt comfortable there, perhaps because his dead father Usir was god of the surrounding thick papyrus. The tiny boy jumped happily along the backs of hippopotami. He grasped the tails of crocodiles and swished through the waters laughing. He wove boats from papyrus reeds and paddled under flapping, funny pelicans. He invited swamp cats to sleep with him on papyrus matting in the daytime. For like those cats, he preferred to be active at night.

There was a reason for this: Life was full of mysteries. He sucked his finger and looked around. He convinced the goddess Nebet Hut to teach him to see in the dark. That way he could defend, against what he knew not, but this ability was crucial. Heru Sa Aset thought of his vision in historic terms: The eye of Heru Sa Aset looked out over the vast maw of the world with knife-edge ferocity.

He fashioned hunting tools—spears, boomerangs, bows and arrows. But the idea of defense, and maybe even offense, lurked persistently.

In a sense the boy had two mothers. One was the wary-eyed Aset, who taught him the rules by which a society runs well, laws his father had given people. She told him, mysteriously, he'd need to know these things. The other mother was the sad-eyed Nebet Hut, aunt and nursemaid. She taught him to take the form of a falcon while she became a

Children and the Law

Ancient texts give us insight into the rights of children during ancient times. For example, in the Bible's Book of Genesis, Cain killed his brother Abel, and in the Book of Matthew King Herod ordered the massacre of male children in Bethlehem. Murder of adults has been illegal probably since the earliest laws. But in the western world it wasn't until the fourth century that law protected a baby. Before that, a father could dispose of a child as he wished.

Egyptian children shown in the marshes with their parents

kite. They swooped over desert and glided on air currents, searching mysteriously. Between the two mothers the workings of the entire cosmos were cloaked in opaque dread.

Once Heru Sa Aset grew to adulthood, he learned the nature of that dread: His uncle Set hated him, simply because he was his father's son. Set had usurped his father's throne. Now Aset wanted Heru Sa Aset to claim it back.

Heru Sa Aset challenged Set valiantly, demanding his due. Set refused, of course. So Heru Sa Aset appealed to the gods' council, the Pesedjet. The god Tehuti urged the Pesedjet to favor Heru Sa Aset. But Set argued that he protected Egypt from foreign enemies; if he were dethroned, Egypt would return to chaos. So the Pesedjet looked like it would find in favor of Set.

Aset thought she'd lose her sanity. She transformed herself into a ravishingly beautiful maiden. The disguised Aset told Set she was a widow, and a stranger had seized her land and threatened her son. She asked his aid.

Anyone in his right mind would have seen how this maiden's story matched Aset's story. But Set wasn't in his right mind. The maiden was luscious; he was hot-blooded. Blind to the trap, he declared this usurper a villain. He swore to fight him and return to the son what was rightfully his.

Aha! Aset revealed her true identity. Aha! The whole

Heru Sa Aset and his uncle Set each suffered brutalities at the hand of the other. But the boy got the worst of it. Fortunately, Hut Heru restored his eyes.

Pesedjet listened. Aha, aha! Set would have to yield now; he had as much as admitted his guilt.

But Set didn't. Battles ensued and persisted for 80 years. Set used brute force in unspeakable ways, including plucking out Heru Sa Aset's eyes, which the goddess Hut Heru, the very eye of Ra, restored by pouring the milk of the starry Milky Way across his brow. Heru Sa Aset used crass trickery. Once he agreed to a boat duel with Set. Both were to use stone boats and try to sink each other. Set's stone boat sank immediately. But Heru Sa Aset's boat was cedar painted to appear stone, so it whipped along until Set, in a rage, turned into a hippo and sank it. Nothing was too low for these gods to stoop to.

At long last, Ra sent a message to Usir in the underworld Duat, beseeching him to end the struggle. Usir sent a return message. The Pesedjet agreed that Heru Sa Aset deserved the throne. Set yielded.

And so Heru Sa Aset wore the red and white crown and ruled all Egypt. People looked to him for guidance in hunting and martial arts, for he had avenged his father against the most frightening of gods, Set.

Avenged his father—ah. Heru Sa Aset didn't know his father. He knew only Usir's story. Now he wanted a filial tie. So he became the link between the world of the living and Duat, accompanying the dead to Usir. Father and son worked together. It felt good. Finally, finally, the sense of dread that Heru Sa Aset had carried almost all his life dissipated.

INPU (ANUBIS)
God of Mummification

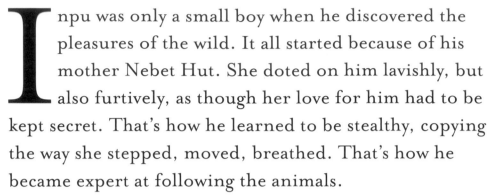

Inpu was only a small boy when he discovered the pleasures of the wild. It all started because of his mother Nebet Hut. She doted on him lavishly, but also furtively, as though her love for him had to be kept secret. That's how he learned to be stealthy, copying the way she stepped, moved, breathed. That's how he became expert at following the animals.

He loved the desert dogs best. Maybe because the dogs themselves were stealthy, that gold fur blending with the sands, even as they worked cooperatively to take down a prey. Or maybe it was because the dogs so obviously enjoyed eating. They even ate fruits, scorned by desert cats. Inpu wasn't omnivorous, of course, but he liked that enthusiasm. Or maybe it was because the dogs had scruples. If they were going to kill an animal to eat, they consistently chose old or sick animals—ones who would die soon anyway. Or newborns. Which might seem gruesome, but, really, newborns were the prey of so many animals; if a mother let her newborn out of sight, the babe was almost sure to get eaten by something. The point was, desert dogs never attacked a strong animal that had a good chance of many more years of life. They weren't ugly about death—they weren't brutal like lions and crocodiles.

Desert dogs ate carrion, too. They gathered at cemeteries and even dug up corpses and ate them. That was hideous, of course. But understandable, given their bestial natures.

The long hours trailing behind desert dogs brought Inpu in contact with death over and over. He thought about it; he dwelled on it. Some deaths seemed almost merciful, some ruthless, some random. He noted that discussions of death are intrinsically intertwined with discussions of life and of how one manages one's way through the ever-changing needs and choices we all face. So it came as no surprise to his parents Set and Nebet Hut when Inpu announced he was going to the underworld Duat to preside over the dead.

Inpu assumed the head of a desert dog and sometimes even the whole body, just in the color black instead of gold. Black was the color of Duat. But it was also the color of the fertile soil along the Nile banks, the soil from which life came. It was the right color. He went about the business

Canines and Felines

Dogs and cats have been pets since ancient times, but they differ in biology and behavior. Dogs belong to the canine family, which is omnivorous. Canines are sociable and cooperative, often living in packs. Cats belong to the feline family, which is carnivorous. Your cat will turn up his nose at pumpkin pie, while your dog will wolf it down. Felines are usually solitary. Cats were sacred to ancient Egyptians; dogs were valued for guarding and hunting.

A wooden sarcophagus showing a man walking his pet dog

of ruling Duat. So far so good, in Inpu's life.

Then, for no reason at all, his father Set killed his truly wonderful uncle Usir, behaving in the most despicable of ways, drawing out the drama like so much ripped flesh. Inpu went fragile inside. He wrinkled his snout, holding in howls of loss and confusion. His aunt Aset—who was beyond compare, the sweet wind that refreshes—plunged into a secretive and solitary state. His own mother Nebet Hut disappeared for long periods. No one seemed to care about Inpu at all. That nearly drove him crazy.

But at least Inpu had his beloved uncle again. Usir came to Duat and Inpu embalmed him himself. Then he behaved as a loyal nephew should: He stepped into the shadows and let his uncle Usir take over the more overarching role.

Inpu, instead, became the patron of orphans and other lost souls. He felt at ease with them, as though he belonged. And he oversaw funeral rites.

Inpu was actually grateful Usir had come to the underworld. Preparing a soul was one thing, judging it was another. Inpu never begrudged abdicating the throne of Duat to Usir.

Inpu was at home in the underworld, serving souls who felt as lost as he had when he walked aboveground, and aiding Usir, his uncle, or maybe, maybe, his father.

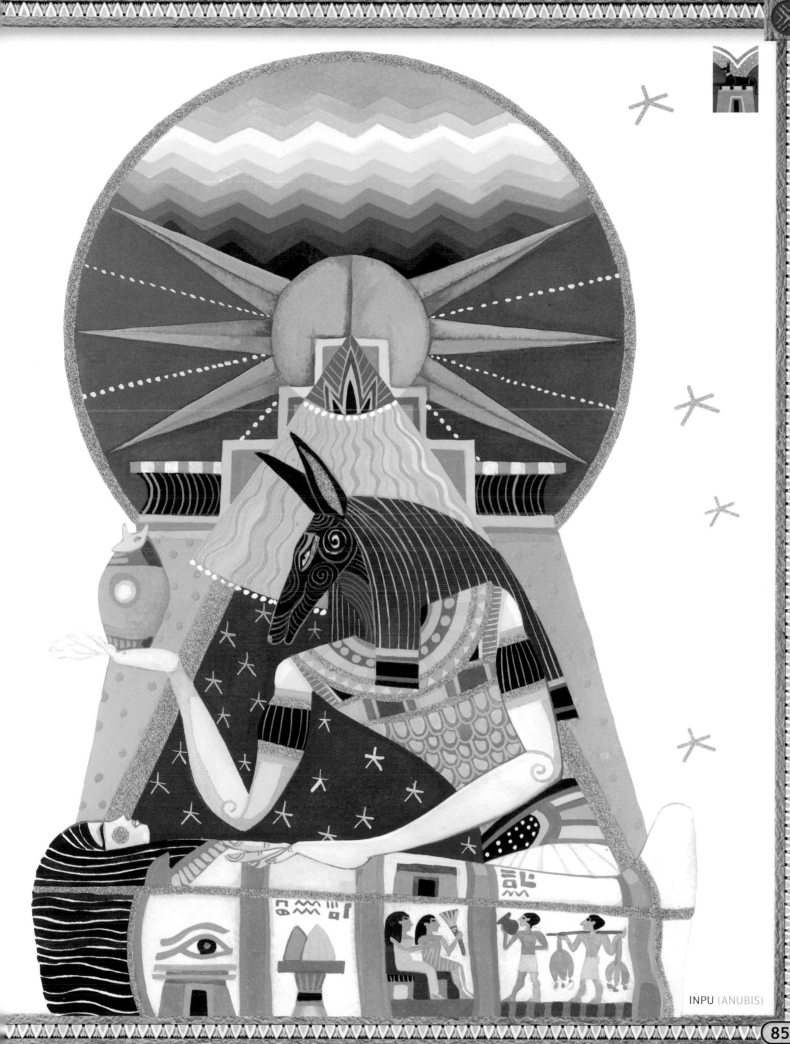

INPU (ANUBIS)

TEFNUT (TPHENIS)
Goddess of Moisture

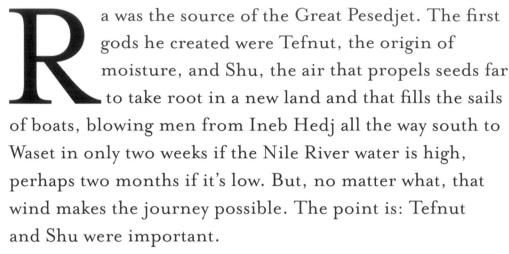

Ra was the source of the Great Pesedjet. The first gods he created were Tefnut, the origin of moisture, and Shu, the air that propels seeds far to take root in a new land and that fills the sails of boats, blowing men from Ineb Hedj all the way south to Waset in only two weeks if the Nile River water is high, perhaps two months if it's low. But, no matter what, that wind makes the journey possible. The point is: Tefnut and Shu were important.

Tefnut and Shu had two children. First, Geb, the earth in all his loamy, wormy fertility, in all his rock that allowed humans to build pyramids, in all his dust and sand that made everyone appreciate the Nile River even more. Second, Nut, the sky who sparkle-danced above, giving that tiny but essential glimmer of hope to human dreams, without which the feebleness of human lives would be brutally exposed, leaving them aghast.

It was only at the next generation down, the great-grandchildren of Ra, that one found Geb and Nut's children: Heru Wer, Usir, Nebet Hut, Set, Aset.

That was the order of things. The structure of the Great Pesedjet made sense time-wise and power-wise. After all, nothing good could happen without air and rain, earth and sky: Shu and Tefnut, Geb and Nut. Yet Tefnut noticed that the ones who got attention were those at the bottom of the Great Pesedjet, that shiftless generation.

Well, Heru Wer, there wasn't much bad to say about him because there wasn't much to say at all. He seemed satisfied playing lackey to Ra.

But Usir, what kind of idiot was he, to climb into that box when Set invited him? Anyone could see it was coffin-size. Anyone could see the glint in Set's eye, the obsession with annihilation.

And Nebet Hut, who could take her seriously? She tricked Usir into fathering her son Inpu—tricked the husband of her sister. All right, all right, so she'd helped Aset to find the pieces of Usir when Set beheaded and dismembered him. But, really now.

And Set. Nothing good could be said about Set.

The only one worth even a spoonful of salt was Aset.

The Smell Culture

Colorful Egyptian perfume bottles on display

Matter consists of particles, and can be solid, liquid, or gas. Many solids are nonvolatile (they don't evaporate), so they have no odor. Others are volatile, allowing you to enjoy the smell of cinnamon, for example. Still, Tefnut is right: Sweetness is a taste, not a smell. Nevertheless, certain odors enhance the perception of sweetness, while others inhibit it. Ancient Egypt had a smell culture: Aromatics included perfumes, spices, rosewater, incense. Good fragrances indicated vitality and morality.

TEFNUT (TPHENIS)

Then Aset made that snake from mixing Ra's drool with clay and got him to reveal his true name to her. Trickery!

Add the five of them together, and what did you have? Stupidity at best and vileness at worst. A slop of deceit and self-centeredness.

That humans should worship them was evidence of idiocy. But now, look what had happened! Just look! Usir had called Aset the sweet wind that refreshes. The name spread. Inpu called her that, then other deities, then humans. And Aset had the nerve to embrace the epithet, as though deserved.

The sweet wind that refreshes. How dare she? Shu was god of good winds. Yes, he'd conceded storms to Set's rule, but that's all—every breeze, every breath came from Shu. And sweetness—everyone knew sweetness was a taste, and taste depended on moisture. So, really, really really really, sweetness belonged to the realm of Tefnut, goddess of moisture.

Furious, Tefnut went straight to Ra. "Do you know what people call Aset now?"

"The sweet wind that refreshes. Justly."

"What? After that stunt she pulled with the snake venom, you should be the last to mouth that epithet."

"It's just a few words."

"Didn't you create the cosmos from words?"

"Let's not quibble, Tefnut. It's evening. I'm tired, little one."

"Don't belittle me. Call me sweet."

"We can't praise both of you for sweetness."

"Then reserve sweet for me. Call me the sweet water that refreshes. No, better, call me the sweet water that gives life."

"Relax, Tefnut. Go rain a while. You need it."

"Me? You're the one who needs it. You'll see!"

Tefnut left in a huff. She ran till her feet were raw like Aset's when she ran after the floating coffin. Tefnut left a bloody trail all the way to Nubia. There she transformed into a lioness, for she and her brother-husband Shu had played lion cubs when small. In this feline body, she could run forever, with the wind whistling past, then run faster until she couldn't hear anything—no epithets at all.

Jealousy, envy, feeling unappreciated—these things reduced Set to a monster, and now they reduced poor Tefnut to a monster. What a pity that gods could lose all perspective.

TEFNUT (TPHENIS)

Appeased by Tehuti's words of adulation, Tefnut let her wrath slip away, and with it went the lioness body. She was, once more, the lovely goddess of moisture.

Egypt grew dry and drier. The sun still crossed the sky—that was Ra's greatest duty, after all—but without moisture, the brilliance blinded, the heat blistered, the dry parched. Tongues swelled, then cracked. Fingernails and claws crusted and crumbled to dust.

Meanwhile Tefnut rampaged through Nubia, causing rain. Nubia flooded while Egypt burned. The lioness grunted, growled, roared; it served them right.

Beside himself, Ra paced as though an idea would come if he kept moving. Tehuti, the tongue of Ra, could barely move from the razor-thin splits across his body. But he forced himself to twist past the pain and speak truth. He called Ra stubborn, foolish. He said sun and moisture needed one another. Hadn't Ra learned anything from Ma'at, the divine order of the cosmos? Tefnut must be lured back to Egypt, before everything and everyone blended with the sands.

Ra listened, with his sliver-thin, dried-out ears. He sent Shu to persuade Tefnut to return. He sent Tehuti, too.

TEFNUT (TPHENIS)

Tehuti could convince anyone of anything.

Tehuti preceded Shu to Nubia. The sight of the lioness shocked him; she was more huge, more terrible than the worst monster. He changed into a baboon, for had he approached the goddess in his godly form, she would have easily slain him. He bounded after her, barking for attention. When she turned to him, he said, "Come home, Tefnut, most honorable one. Come home to the comforts of Egypt."

Her yellow eyes bore into him. She stepped forward.

Tehuti thought of honey, of warm summer rain, of survival. "Egypt loves you, most honorable one. Egypt needs you, most honorable one. Egypt misses you."

"Say it," rumbled Tefnut.

"Most honorable one."

Tefnut shed her feline body and accompanied Shu and Tehuti to Egypt, where she was known ever after as the most honorable one.

Fitting. In a land of desert, the goddess of moisture is the most honorable one.

TEFNUT (TPHENIS)

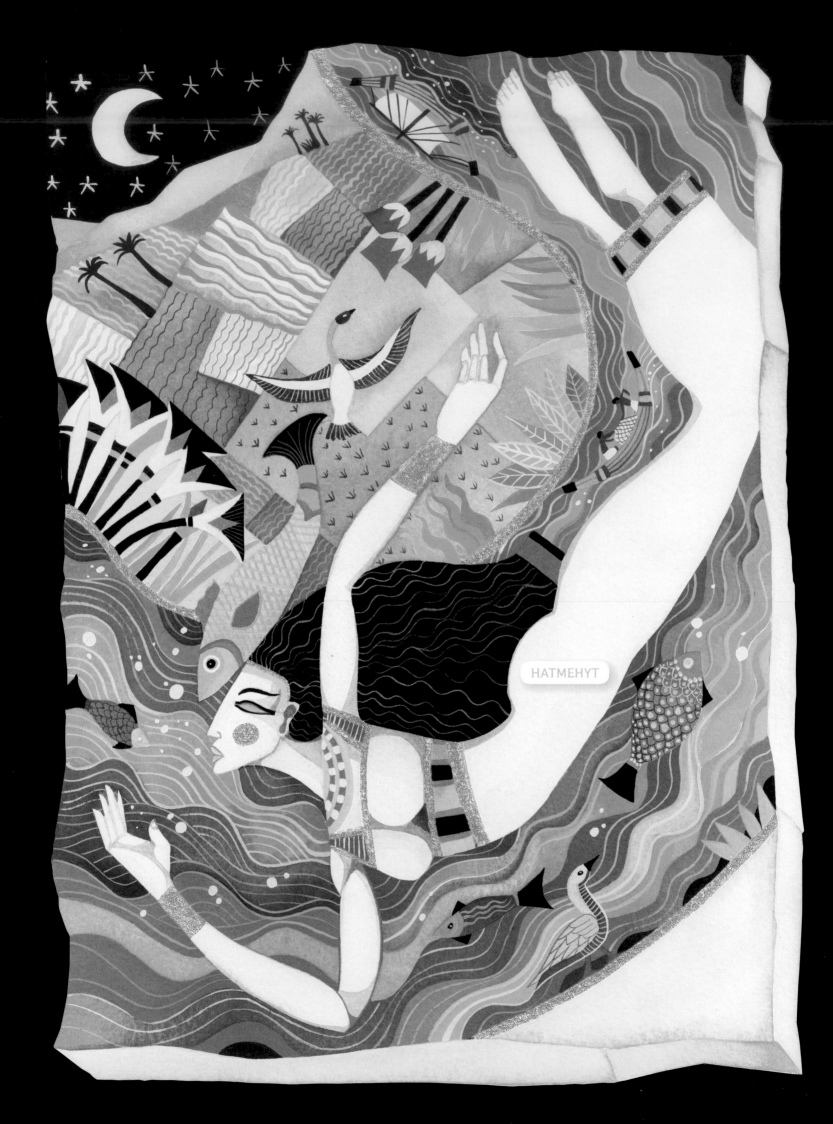

THE GREAT NILE
The Source of So Much

While life started from the amorphous waters of Nun, the Nile River was, in a practical and daily way, an equally important source of life. For one, the Nile quenched thirst. When Tefnut ran from Egypt and left the country without rainfall, the Nile saved the population from fatal dehydration.

For another, the Nile housed fish. Some were considered sacred and there was even a fish goddess, Hatmehyt, *(see illustration, left)* worshipped in the delta. And because a fish had eaten the fourteenth part of Usir (a fish that many believed to be wicked Set himself), some people had a fear of eating them and perhaps eating that fourteenth part. So priests never ate fish and rich people often saw them only as pretty things for decorative pools. Yet, among the masses fish were a dietary staple, luckily, because even the poorest could fish, and the nutritional value of Nile fish, such as the abundant tilapia, was high. Fishermen used nets or a fish hook on a string—an angle— often made of mussel shell. The art of angling might well have originated in Egypt. Fishermen also used the aid of cormorants or similar birds—just as in China, Japan, and Macedonia. They put a loop around the bird's throat, then they set the bird free. When the bird caught tiny fish, it could swallow them. But if it caught a big fish, it had to return to the fisherman for help. The fisherman would take the fish from the bird's mouth and give the bird a piece small enough to swallow as payment.

The Nile and the sun defined Egypt, one fertilizing the land and watering the plants, the other supplying heat and light. The pyramids, symbols of the pharaoh, watched it all.

The Nile played a crucial role in agriculture. The seasons that Ra governed marked times of different agricultural behavior of the Nile. One season was the inundation: The waters rose over the riverbanks to flood the land between June or July and September or October. As they gradually receded, they deposited sediment, making the land fertile and soft for cultivation. Next came the growing season. Farmers grew beans and grapes. They grew barley and wheat to make bread. Then they crumpled old bread into water and made beer, their most common drink, the beverage Hut Heru urged on them to lessen anxieties so they could enjoy music and dance. All this was possible because farmers irrigated fields with small canals dug out to the now calm Nile. Finally came harvest season, when the abundant food could be transported easily up and down the Nile. The Nile, the Nile, in every season, the Nile.

Aset's tears when Set nailed her husband Usir into the carved box caused the first flooding. Usir surveyed the cycle those tears set in motion and decided to give people

the gift of flooding annually—a resurrection of the land to commemorate his own resurrection.

The Nile played a part in hunting, too. The floodwaters filled indentations in the land that were then cut off from the river when the tide lowered: hence many inland ponds. These became water holes for land animals, such as gazelles, deer, ostrich. They formed refuges for birds, which nested on islands in the center. Hunters erected reed blinds to wait for thirsty animals, and then took them down with spears, bows and arrows, lassos, and boomerangs that Heru Sa Aset taught them to make. Hunters caught birds at these flood pools, too—coot, ducks, geese. Sometimes pool fish multiplied so exuberantly that people snatched small fish in their hands—a quick dinner.

Another product of flooding was the formation of clay. The god Khnum made a potter's wheel and fashioned humans from that clay. When he showed humans how to make wheels, they crafted household pottery and decorative containers for use in temples. Clay served as mortar between the blocks of

Slings and spears were the first projectile weapons, but bows and arrows have been used for millennia. The bow above is made of antelope horns connected by a central piece of wood.

Often pots had a tapered or even pointed end, so that they could be pushed into the dirt or sand and stand on their own to be used for storage.

the step pyramids. Homes were made of sun-baked bricks, but often the walls were smeared with plaster so that they could be painted. The first layer of plaster was formed from river clay. Sometimes a second layer of gypsum plaster was applied. Pharaohs' tombs and gods' temples were made glorious, thanks to clay. Nile clays could be used in all these ways because they contained lime, a natural binder. And they were known for high plasticity, which allowed potters to make unusual-shaped pots that were traded along the Nile and beyond.

The Nile also supplied two of the most important symbols of Egypt: the lotus for Upper Egypt and the papyrus for Lower Egypt. Aset loved that flower for its scent. And Usir loved that reed for its strength. It was perfect that their son Heru Sa Aset was born in the delta region, itself shaped like a lotus blossom and thick with reeds. Aset and Hut Heru taught humans the joys of lotus perfumes and oils. Hut Heru and the serpent goddess Wadjet taught them the versatility of the papyrus. People wove reed mats, baskets, sandals, blankets. They made papyrus ropes for

use in beds and for animal tethers. They burned papyrus for cooking and heating, and used the ashes to cure mouth sores, eye inflammations, and skin ailments. They ate the lower parts raw or roasted. They made paper and, with Tehuti's instruction, they wrote tales on scrolls they stored in chests. To bolster their commerce, they built boats. Egypt had few trees, so these reed boats offered inexpensive transportation on the river. Going north, the light boats skimmed with the current, helped by paddles and poles. Going south, a raised sail—usually made of woven reeds, naturally—caught wind from the Mediterranean Sea and so the boats skimmed just as fast, even against the current.

The Nile River teemed with hippopotami and crocodiles, ruled by the goddess Taweret and the god Sobek. It was a sacred home, to be revered. When Usir became ruler of the underworld, he had the goddess Satet, Khnum's wife, purify corpses with water from the Nile's source.

It's no wonder, then, that the ancients built temples to the Nile at Ineb Hedj (Memphis), Iunu (Heliopolis), and Delas (Nilopolis), almost as though the river itself were a god.

> To make papyrus, strips of plant stalk were pounded side by side. The next layer was placed at a right angle and pounded again. Sugar within the reed sealed the strips together.

THE GREAT NILE

TEHUTI (THOTH)
God of Knowledge

I t's not easy being Ra's tongue, Tehuti could attest to
that. Others interpreted his words as the sun god's
wishes alone, as though Tehuti were but an instrument.
The truth was, without Tehuti, Ra couldn't make
it through a day. Tehuti stood at the prow of the boat *Manjet*
as it crossed the sky, while Ra went from being a newborn
hardly bigger than a scarab hatching from dung, to a youth
strong and bold as a falcon, to an old man the wind could
toss. So Tehuti's responsibility for guiding the boat expanded
as the daylight shrank.

Oh, Tehuti wasn't alone in that job. Ma'at, the spirit
of cosmic balance and a child of Ra, also rode the boat.
Though the goddess Ma'at was only an idea, she supported
Tehuti in tasks. Tehuti loved Ma'at as his partner. In a
sense, they were wed.

Others sometimes entered the boat—gods, animals—but
as passengers, along for the ride.

In evening, Ma'at shared a dreadful task with Tehuti.
That's when the old man Ra traveled the twelve caverns of the
underworld Duat in the boat *Mesektet,* going now from west

Apep is the beast
that inhabits our
worst nightmares.
And he was that
to Ra, as well, for
he reappeared
every night, threat-
ening shipwreck
and, thus, the end
of time.

to east. Hungry serpentine monsters infested the waters, and the old man Ra was too feeble, in body and heart, to conquer them. Ma'at spied the monsters; Tehuti veered around them.

But every night when they reached the ninth cavern, Apep attacked. Apep was the worst creature imaginable, without eyes, ears, nose. Nothing scared this nearly insensate demon. His breath was a roar of terror. Nightly Ra and Ma'at and Tehuti fought Apep until Apep sprayed poison into Ra's eyes. Then Tehuti wiped Ra's eyes clear so he could spear Apep through his iron scales into his pitiless heart; the monster's blood then spurted up and up and colored the sky rosy, the backdrop for Ra's reappearance as newborn dawn.

Tehuti sang his victory, like baboons sing at the rising sun. Sometimes he got so carried away he took baboon form himself.

The god Set claimed it was he who fought Apep each night, the liar. The vanquishing of darkness, the coming of light—all that depended on Tehuti.

TEHUTI (THOTH)

And it wasn't just the day's cycle that Tehuti ensured; he made the year's cycle work. In the beginning, the year was 360 days, and the waters of Nun were sterile. But Tehuti played a high-stakes dice game with the moon god Khonsu. He won, and got a seventy-secondth of the moon's light: five days. Over those days, Nun was fertile; the first deities were created. In gratitude to Khonsu, Tehuti curved his ibis bill to match the crescent moon's shape.

Looked at from a certain perspective then, Tehuti was creator of the cosmos, not Ra. Tehuti would never voice this, of course. But facts were facts.

Tehuti served whoever needed him. He was aware of what could go wrong—he heard the waiting phantoms of pandemonium calmly licking their chops. Their appetites must never be satiated.

Tehuti convinced Tefnut to come back to Egypt after Ra had refused to show her fair appreciation. He spoke with reason; that's all it took.

It was Tehuti, always Tehuti, who solved the problem, whatever the problem. When Set ripped Usir into 14 pieces and Aset could find only 13, Tehuti whispered to her sounds to make Usir whole and alive long enough to conceive Heru Sa Aset. Then he protected Aset during pregnancy. And when Heru Sa Aset fought with Set for 80 years, Tehuti maintained the power balance. If one gravely injured the other, Tehuti's

Hieroglyph Records

Tax records in hieroglyphs date back to 3300 B.C., and many later hieroglyphs exist as well. But scholars could not decipher them. Then in 1799 scholars studied a stone slab with parallel texts in Greek, Demotic (the script of late Egyptian), and hieroglyphs. The first two scripts helped decipher hieroglyphs. Some hieroglyphs stood for sounds, some stood for meanings, and some distinguished between homophones. That's why the code was hard to crack—it was complex.

The Rosetta Stone inscribed with ancient Egyptian hieroglyphs, among other writings

words healed the underdog. Once Tehuti recovered all but a small fraction of the eye Set had gouged out of Heru Sa Aset, and once he brought fatally wounded Heru Sa Aset back to life. Tehuti restored order. That was the bottom line. He honored Ma'at; Tehuti was god of wisdom.

In his wisdom he gave people words, to philosophize and pray. He gave them hieroglyphs, to record when, where, why, how, who—to keep track of history. He taught them numbers to calculate the layout of the heavens, the stars, the earth, and all within them, and to understand astronomy. He helped them look around objectively, so they could know—not just imagine; he gave them science.

One might conclude Tehuti was the most important god—for isn't wisdom the most important virtue? And if one did, Tehuti might agree. But he would never say it; he was far too wise.

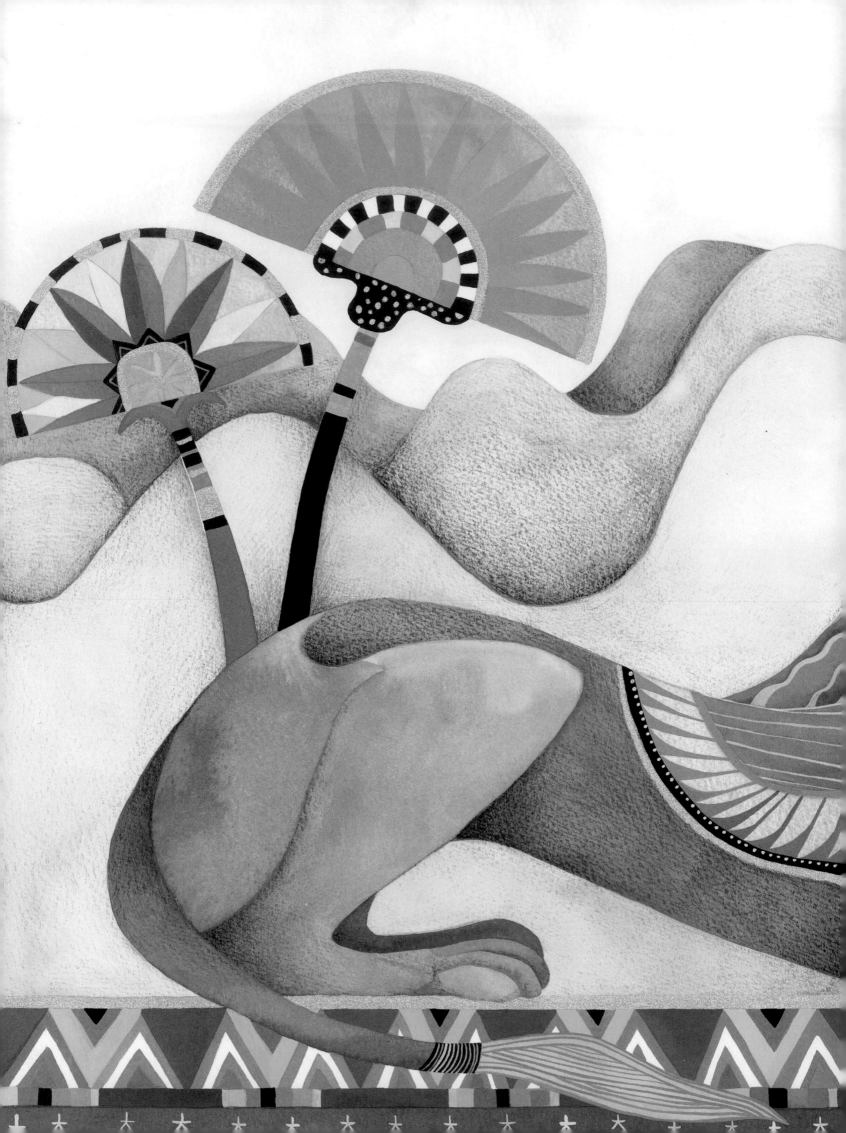

HERU WER (HORUS THE ELDER)
Winged Sun Disk and Protector of Egypt

In the beginning . . . ah, many stories open that way. They say in the beginning there was water. What? In the beginning there was nothing. Imagine it, if you can. Can you? Really? The idea of nothingness confounds most of us—it is chaos, literally. So we replace it with water, essential to life as we know it. We pretend that in the beginning there was the vast amorphous Nun. Next came heat and light, of course, in the form of the sun god Ra. Ra says he quickly had nine progeny: Shu and Tefnut, their children Geb and Nut, and their children Nebet Hut, Set, Aset, Usir, and Heru Wer.

But Heru Wer would tell a different story.

First, though, take another look. What kind of name is that: Heru Wer—Horus the Elder? It's as though this god didn't get named until after his nephew Heru was born. At first the boy's name seemed homage to a revered uncle. But then Heru Sa Aset entered that interminable war with Set and made a name for himself—drowning out his uncle's name.

When people spoke of Heru, Heru Wer wasn't sure whether they spoke of him or his nephew. How annoying. His siblings basked in the brightness of their fame or infamy. But Heru Wer was hidden in the shade of the younger Heru Sa Aset. Bah!

Everything was flawed.

The creation story was the most flawed. Heru Wer felt ancient. Perhaps he'd had a prior life as war god, before the beginning of time, somewhere other than Egypt? His heart belonged across the sea, near mountains and a river, maybe in lands to the east. Some other world.

But here he was—in this world—and no one paid attention. Tefnut complained no one appreciated her and threw a tantrum that seared Egypt almost to death. It ended in Tefnut's being called the most honorable one. Tehuti complained of being unappreciated, though behind Ra's back. Yet Tehuti rode in Ra's boat—what higher place of honor? Their wrongs were nothing compared with being outshone by a whippersnapper nephew!

Well, Heru Wer deserved honor. He was falcon, searching for prey over relentless, scorching sands. He was lion, blending with dry acacia, then bounding out to stun the unwary. He was prince of gods, guiding the pharaoh in whispers. He was all three, in sphinx form.

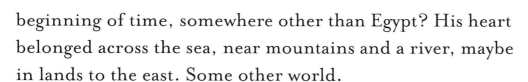

Gods of Ancient Lands

In prehistory the scattered people in Egypt worshipped natural phenomena, seeing divinity in earth, sky, rain, sun, animals. As ancient Egypt grew, new villages added new gods. In those times there was little threat from invaders, so Egyptian mythology developed independently. Still, there is similarity between Heru Wer as a war god who also protected the peace and the god Nergal of the Babylonians. Whether one has its origins in the other is an open question.

Wall decorations at the Horus Temple in Egypt tell stories of the gods.

Heru Wer was the sky's face. When he opened his right eye, the sun glared. When he opened his left, the moon glowed. Heru Wer gave organization to time, not Ra. Ra merely crossed the sky in a boat. But Heru Wer fought off Set's storms that otherwise could have poked out Ra's eyes and clouded the earth forever. Some even said Heru Wer was Ra-Herakhty—Ra at midday, his strongest.

So when Set gathered an army and declared war, Ra rightly turned to Heru Wer for help. Set said Ra was weak and old and he, mighty Set, should become king of gods. Set always was a pompous bully. Heru Wer came quickly to defend Ra. Besides, Set had killed his brother Usir; Heru Wer wanted revenge.

Heru Wer was no fool. So he went to Tehuti for a spell that turned him into a winged sun disk. He blazed above Set's army, befuddling their sight and hearing. The blighted soldiers thought enemies surrounded them. They threw themselves upon one another, bludgeoning, stabbing, slashing, until all lay slain upon sands stained blood-red forever after. Heru Wer hovered over the corpses, looking for Set. In vain.

So Heru Wer went back to Ra, and they traveled down the Nile.

But Set was crafty in warfare; he had saved soldiers aside, still alive. He commanded them to transform into

hippopotami and crocodiles, and attack Ra's boat. The benevolent hippo goddess Taweret, who walked on two feet with pregnant belly, couldn't control these faux hippos. Sobek, the croc god, was likewise stumped.

Who came to the rescue? Heru Wer! He anticipated trouble; with Tehuti's help he had armed Ra's men with magic lances and chains. They killed the hippos and crocs.

Set sent more soldier hippos and crocs. Heru Wer killed many and took prisoners. He again assumed the form of a winged sun disk and pursued the remaining soldiers into the desert, where he slew some and captured others.

Set, senseless with evil, hid in serpent form.

Heru Wer stayed alert in case Set thought of returning. No one would ever get the better of Heru Wer.

That's who Heru Wer was: defender of Egypt, war god, the power behind it all.

The god Heru Wer became a winged sun disk, blinding Set's soldiers with his brightness, so that they mistook one another for enemies and caused their own slaughter.

HERU WER (HORUS THE ELDER)

HUT HERU (HATHOR)
Goddess of Delights

People liked to talk, often without much to say. But sometimes chattering went beyond thoughtless, to reckless. The sun god Ra was leader, and talking about him was a common pastime. They heard about how Ra battled with Apep and needed Tehuti's help to survive his passage through the underworld each night. They heard about how Ra drooled and Aset created a serpent from that spittle to bite him and trick him into revealing his secret name.

"See? Don't you see?" they said. Ra wasn't half the god he used to be. Before, he was invincible and astute.

There was no doubt about it, said the people. Ra had grown infirm. No brawn, no vigor. He should be replaced.

Ra was furious, naturally. He had faced that very challenge from the god Set and enlisted the help of Heru Wer to meet it. But now to be challenged by mere humans? Outrageous! He sent for his eye, the goddess Hut Heru, to punish the humans.

Hut Heru stood as though struck by lightning. Why had Ra chosen her? Hut Heru had no experience with punishment.

The vast waters of Nun from which Ra had first risen moved quickly sometimes, forming a tide called Mehet-Weret. Each dawn Mehet-Weret helped Ra rise from the waters of the underworld up into the current of the sky to begin a new day. Mehet-Weret was like a loving mother to Ra; she came in cow form, a sun disk between her horns. Stars twinkled from her ears. Mehet-Weret splashed up and

Dance for all Occasions

Hut Heru was goddess of many things, including the important art of dance. At funerals ancient Egyptians danced in serpentine lines to ward off evil spirits. The pharaoh performed the sun dance and his priests performed fertility dances. Warriors danced as a group, with individuals competing in mock battles. At festivals and banquets, pairs of skilled dancers performed. Ordinary people did circle dances to celebrate daily life. Movements ranged from dignified walking to acrobatic tricks.

A scene from an Egyptian tomb shows women dancing and playing music.

kissed the Milky Way, which was Hut Heru's special sparkle. Hut Heru loved Mehet-Weret in return, and was inspired to move fluids, too. She poured the milk of the Milky Way onto Heru Sa Aset and restored the young god's eyes after his uncle Set had plucked them out. She made the waters inside a pregnant woman roil and burst forth to announce an imminent birth.

Hut Heru stayed beside the women through labor, delivery, and the child's infancy. She didn't usurp Nebet Hut's role as comforter in birthing pains. She didn't usurp Aset's role as fertility goddess and family adviser. Instead, she complemented them. These goddesses worked together for women's health and joy.

Hut Heru found delight in bodily senses. She loved perfume and had people burn myrrh incense in her honor. Fragrances gave pleasure to breathing, so Hut Heru's gift to the nose was felt with every inhalation.

She loved the colors of stones and metals: turquoise, malachite, gold, copper. She became patron goddess of miners and urged people to wear jewelry, even slaves. She taught women to grind malachite into powder to circle their eyes and appear beautiful. The powder protected against infection, so the women could enjoy the pleasures of sight their whole life. Gifts to the eyes.

Hut Heru played the harp exquisitely. And she had a favorite turquoise necklace, the *menat,* which she shook as she danced, to make a tinkly noise that brought smiles. Her laughter, too, was musical—a gift to the ears.

She danced when her father Ra was despondent, danced and danced till he couldn't help but smile. She took people's hands and taught them choral dances, stamping to the sistrum beats. Another gift—this time to the sense of rhythm that comes from the heart.

She gave people wine and beer, for alcohol loosened their limbs to dance and released them from worry.

From the moment Ra created her, Hut Heru knew she was counted on. She listened carefully; she came when prayed to or sung to or even thought about.

This was who Hut Heru was: the goddess who taught women delight.

HUT HERU (HATHOR)

And now Ra, of whom she was the very eye, asked her to take vengeance on humans? She didn't know where to begin.

But then the ugly rumors against Ra entered her ears and bounced inside her head, then descended into her heart and crashed like the cymbals *sekhem*. Thorns of anger poked the back of her eyes. Fury set her heart afire. Her hair grew into a gold lion mane. Her fingernails became claws, her teeth, fangs. Her gentle face transformed into the visage of wrath.

Hut Heru roared and sprang after those who had maligned Ra. They fled into the desert and hid among rocks. She shredded them. She ran into villages and slew humans who had never spoken even one evil word against Ra. The Nile foamed red with the blood of innocents.

That night Hut Heru returned to Ra. He praised her. "We have prevailed, because of you, Hut Heru. Rest now. You deserve it. Rest."

But she didn't.
She couldn't.

Any lion will kill if hungry or threatened. But this lioness killed for the sake of slaughter itself, trapped in a frenzy fueled by rage.

HUT HERU (HATHOR)

SEKHMET (SACHMIS)
Goddess of Vengeance

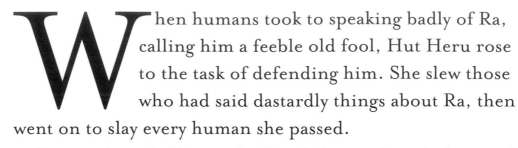

When humans took to speaking badly of Ra, calling him a feeble old fool, Hut Heru rose to the task of defending him. She slew those who had said dastardly things about Ra, then went on to slay every human she passed.

Ra was pleased. He stood tall and the wind swirled around him in a great funnel up into the sky forever. He assumed yet another name now, Amun-Ra, god of victory, war lord. This is what the people of the strong town Waset, known for ferocity in war, had been calling him for years, and they had built him and his wife Mut the most splendid temple ever. Amun-Ra shouted, "On, on!" People must fear him. All nations must come under his sway. They must make sacrifices to him. Give up the throne? Never! Amun-Ra would be the true father of every future pharaoh. He would from then on assume the outward appearance of the reigning pharaoh and walk boldly into the sleeping queen's chambers and leave her perfumed and lovely . . . and with child. Each queen would rejoice in her love for him. All would be perfect. Feeble old fool—ha! Amun-Ra would show them. Every pharaoh from that moment on would be the earthly embodiment of Amun-Ra himself. When they died, they'd rejoin Amun-Ra in the sky. Nothing could be more perfect.

And the goddess Hut Heru had helped to assure this future. She was splendid.

Except now that victory was his, Amun-Ra wanted Hut Heru to stop the slaughter. The sight of all that carnage turned even his stomach. But she wouldn't. Hut Heru hunted with the lethal speed of a lioness. Hot winds skimmed the desert, picking up sand and grinding them into people's flesh, and the people screamed, sure that these scouring, scaring winds were the breath of the angry goddess. They called her Sekhmet now, the powerful one, the dread-bearer.

Wrath made Sekhmet blood-crazed. She was vengeance incarnate. Death seemed attracted to her. Whenever she stopped, even for a moment, vipers clustered around and twined upward, forming writhing anklets and bracelets, increasing the tremors the sight of her caused. She was isolated, a pride of one, yet more effective than a dozen lions. This was right, this was as it should be, these people had insulted

The Afterlife

The idea of balance, embodied in Ma'at, appears in the Book of the Dead, which lists reasons souls can be rejected from the afterlife, including offenses of imbalance: falsehoods, prolonged grief, boasting, unkindness to animals, polluting river water. Still, society was riddled with the crimes of ordinary people and pharaohs, some of whom were infamous for oppression. So the duality of Hut Heru—Sekhmet may reflect the difficulty people recognized in following their own ethic.

Papyrus from the Book of the Dead, which was first developed in the ancient city of Waset

Amun-Ra, they were slime. They deserved to perish in hideous ways, torn limb from limb, eaten alive, their shrieks cut off as her jaw clamped around their throats. This was divine justice. Let their blood feed the crops. Let it nourish the land. Let it pour.

Ra watched in horror. If Sekhmet wasn't stopped, there would be no people left to serve him. What was wrong with her?

He called gods and people together and they brewed barrels and barrels of the strongest beer known to anyone. Seven thousand barrels. Then Ra had them grind up ochre clay and crush hibiscus petals and squash pomegranates to add red coloring and fragrance and taste. He had them mash in poppy and mandrake, to make the brew even stronger— strong enough to overwhelm Sekhmet's senses. They worked through the long night.

Blood is nourishment to a lion, yet Sekhmet's thirst went far beyond the need for drink. It was an obsession, and only its satisfaction could free the gentle Hut Heru within.

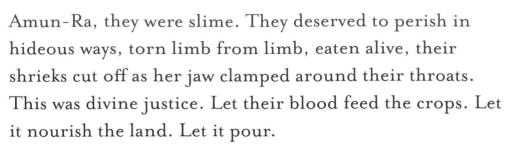

SEKHMET (SACHMIS)

Before daylight, as Sekhmet slept, they poured this most special beer across the earth. They flooded the fields, just as the Nile did annually. But they flooded the valleys, too.

In the morning, Sekhmet rose, eager for the hunt, her mouth dripping with need, her heart rock-dry. People—she would devour them all! Then, oh, the dawn glinted rosy off the new sea before her. She jumped to her feet and turned in a circle. Was this an enormous moat of blood? Had she spilled all that in her rampage the day before? How gratifying!

Sekhmet leaned over and saw her own visage mirrored in the slightly effervescent surface. Her crimson-reflected feline tongue dipped tentatively; sweet, dense drops clung to its barbs. She dipped that tongue again. Delicious. She slurped faster. She slurped all morning, all noon, all night. Her need was satiated and still she drank, unable to stop. Slurp and slurp. Her belly swelled till it could no more, and she swooned headfirst into the small remaining puddle.

Slowly she looked around. Everything blurred, but gradually lines grew sharp. What was she doing here, lying in this sloshy clay? She glimpsed a movement—over there, behind a boulder. A person had peeked out at her, then quickly hidden in fear. Whatever for? People had no reason to fear Hut Heru. The goddess stood up, and the

SEKHMET (SACHMIS)

lioness body that had enveloped her through the bloody frenzy shed away like fog dissipating before sunbeams.

Hut Heru walked forward, the gentle one, Ra's trusted eye.

But Sekhmet existed now—the other aspect of Hut Heru— the fire-spitting eye of Ra, the solar lady of flame that seared everyone at midday. This Sekhmet was the abyss of all fears since the beginning of time, while Hut Heru was love incarnate. That duality felt natural to Sekhmet–Hut Heru; together they were a balance of nature, as Ma'at preached. At the call of divine justice, Sekhmet could spring forth as lioness, ever-ready to protect Egypt against enemies from within or without.

But she could also appear just because she wanted to. That was the beauty of existence. Random, rogue, freak.

And she wanted to now. She looked at Ra and she saw him in her own way, as her own idea of the creator god. She called him Ptah—yet another identity for Ra—and she took him to the town of Ineb Hedj and married him. The people of Ineb Hedj believed Ptah rose from the watery mass of Nun and created the world and all sense of time, though he himself was immeasurable. But they said it was a separate god Ra who drove the sunlight across the sky each day. And they said it was another god, Khnum, who fashioned humans out of clay on his potter's wheel. This was fine with Sekhmet; Ptah pleased her, whatever his powers were, whatever other gods he might overlap with.

SEKHMET (SACHMIS)

Sekhmet plucked a blue lotus from the primeval sea of Nun and held it to Ptah's nose. Behold, out stepped their son Nefertem, who ever after wore on his head a blue lotus bloom with two plumes rising up. And now there were three again: Ptah, Sekhmet, and Nefertem—a triad in charge of Ineb Hedj.

It felt right. It felt healed. And so Sekhmet willed herself to become the goddess of healing. She could banish plague. She could save the wounded. She could be as good as she wanted.

But always in the back of her heart there scrabbled a force that could destroy.

Flowers precede fruit, of course, but that a child should come from a flower simply out of a mother's holding the sweet bloom to the father's nose is a numinous delight indeed.

SEKHMET (SACHMIS)

Warrior Goddess and Weaver of the Cosmos

NIT (NEITH)

Warrior Goddess and Weaver of the Cosmos

There's more to every story than meets the eye. It isn't simply that some things are invisible (which they surely are). And it isn't simply that the eye is sometimes blind (which it surely can be, by choice or by being duped). It's that stories have so many sides, it's impossible to see every facet at once. And it's that stories evolve over time, telling and retelling themselves, becoming and re-becoming in ways we might not have anticipated originally but that ultimately feel inevitable.

That's why it's easy to fail to see Nit. She is herself and at the same time she is facets of so many other gods and goddesses. Nit is elusive.

Life needs a source. In the beginning, the primordial waters of Nun parted as the god Ra created himself through words. Yet, still, this self-generation was within the lapping wetness of Nun. Nun was his source.

Ra went on to create others—all on his own, without a partner. So he tells us. But, really? Did he really do it all on his own? Nun couldn't bear to leave the rest of creation entirely up to the sun god. Ra was a burly fellow, a shouter, indefatigable, and somewhat blunt. These qualities could be assets in many situations, but not all. He needed the help of Nun's feminine aspects. He needed the help of Nit, that more subtle side of Nun.

Nit was self-begotten, just as Ra was—but again, she came from Nun, she had a source. And she formed herself as a

Fine Clothing

Hemp and flax are indigenous to Egypt and were used as far back as the Neolithic period (9500 B.C.) for weaving clothing. Ancient Egyptians herded sheep and spun woolen coats. Silk (originally from China) came to Egypt at least by the first century B.C.; Queen Cleopatra is known for silk garments. Today Egypt is famous for cotton clothing, but cotton (originally from India) came to Egypt via Nubia and wasn't used in clothing until A.D. 125 or later.

Colorful woven cloth in an open-air market

wise one. What was the point of doing otherwise, after all?

She was immediately respected for her wisdom. When the god Heru Sa Aset, the son of the goddess Aset and the god Usir, fought with his uncle god Set, Nit was called upon at one point as arbiter. Nit took the side of Heru Sa Aset; it was his right to inherit his father's throne. But she recommended that Set receive compensation; he'd already usurped the throne, so he was being forced to abnegate it. That smarted, and that meant compensation could help. She said Set should be given the two Syrian war goddesses, Astarte and Anat, as wives. That wasn't the end of the conflict, of course—it went on and on for years. But it could have been, if Set hadn't been stubborn and had listened to the wisdom of Nit. In this way Nit was like a side of the god Tehuti, Ra's tongue and the champion of reason and balance.

Nit guided women at the loom so well that Egypt became known not just for the gauze that wrapped mummies, but for all cloth. Even today Egyptian woven goods are prized.

NIT (NEITH)

There was something commanding about Nit, something that made you pay attention. She was determined to create, and so she picked up the weaver's loom—the most prized possession of women—and she wove and wove. Some say Nit wove the world. But she didn't need people to believe such a grandiose thing. She was satisfied with women weavers honoring her. She paid them back by offering her protection. She extended that protection to all married women. In this way she was not just a side of Nun and of Tehuti, she was a side of the gentle, loving goddess Hut Heru.

Nit had a core of pity that looked at the loom and realized there were others she could help. So she wove and wove again. She wove the white linen swaths that circled bodies in mummification. This was her gift to the dead. And she took special interest in the innards of the dead, for it was often injuries to the torso that caused death—injuries in battle.

Nit cared about battle injuries because she was goddess of war. "How?" one might ask. "How could a goddess protect married women and at the same time lead their men into the dangers of war?" But look again. Look as hard as you can. Nit looked hard. She knew there would always be enemies, always be threats. War could be an evil in itself, but it might also be a response to threats. War was complex. So Nit was a side of the ruthless, furious goddess Sekhmet.

The goddess Hut Heru and the goddess Sekhmet were two sides of a single coin, but they walked separately, with different faces and names. The goddess Nit, instead, was the whole coin, good and evil inextricably intertwined. And she felt more whole than anyone, for that's the way the world was, as she saw it—not one color, not just bad or good, but the whole rainbow, the whole span from decent to indecent.

Nit wore a shield that some thought was the figure eight on its side. Others thought it was a symbol for the infinite. But, in fact, it was the outline of two click beetles head to head. Nit loved the click beetle. It was less showy than the scarab, so dear to Ra. Nit liked modesty. But, even better, the click beetle surprised you. Whenever it wanted, it could flip through the air with a loud click and wind up far from where it started. Nit loved that fact; life was surprising, after all. Life could fling itself this way and that, leaving you searching for what you thought was right in front of you a moment before, leaving you wondering what was reality and what was illusion.

Maybe it was because of her role as goddess of war and maybe not, but Nit also became goddess of the hunt. She helped men spot prey and take them down. This was one more way she protected marriages: Families got fed.

She had her own marriage; she was wife to the god Khnum. Soon she was mother to two sons. One was the crocodile god Sobek, and she nursed him with love, which

may be why this beast never became cruel. The other was
the god Apep, who arose by accident when Nit spat into the
waters of Nun. Apep immediately dove to the underworld
abyss, as the serpentine demon that attacked Ra's boat
Mesektet every night and got speared, his blood splashing
everywhere, only to mend and then fight the same battle
the next night. That both her children belonged to the
water made sense—Nit was an extension of Nun. That one
lived above and one lived below also made sense—Nit was
always a mix, always half this and half that. Aren't we all?

Nit could nurture
. . . and punish;
she gave birth
to a god who did
much good and to
one who did evil;
she was a mix, a
surprise, a tough
one to pin down.

KHNUM (CHNOUMIS)
God of the Potter's Wheel

The god Khnum was the husband of Nit. They lived together in the city Ta-senet. Sometimes, that is, for Nit was just one of Khnum's wives.

At the island Abu, far south in Upper Egypt, Khnum had a wife named Satet. Satet was no slouch. As Ra's daughter she was so fine an archer that she was the local hunting goddess. She helped Khnum in his task as guardian of the Nile's source in the underworld. She helped so much, some say she was the Nile guardian. And since the Nile's flooding ensured fertile soil for the next planting, and that planting and harvest, in turn, ensured human survival, Satet strutted proudly, with ostrich plumes in her crown. She was as much a fertility goddess as Hut Heru. Her daughter, Anuket, stayed at her side or took the form of a gazelle and raced south through beautiful Nubia, where she was a favored goddess. So Khnum had a satisfied and satisfying life in Abu.

At the town Her-wer Khnum had another wife: Heket. Often thousands of frogs gathered on the Nile banks to praise Heket, the frog goddess of creation. You see, Khnum was the great creator; the job was a natural for him, because he had the materials right at hand. After flooding, when the Nile waters receded, they left behind silts and marls—the basics of clay. Khnum invented the potter's wheel and formed humans from clay. Then Heket hopped in, as frogs will do. She breathed life into the little bodies and tucked them inside their mothers' womb. She did this even to the children of the wicked pharaoh Khufu, who was building greater pyramids than anyone before him, but who showed little mercy to his people. Heket was merciful, though. Pregnant women knew Heket had helped to start the life within them, and they counted on her. They wore frog amulets to protect them through gestation. And near labor time, they begged Heket to start the work and assist in the delivery. In this way she was like the goddess Nebet Hut. Again, Khnum had chosen well—this partner wife gave people breath so that Khnum's creation of them led to true life.

And in the city Ta-senet, along with Nit, Khnum had two other wives: Menhit and Nebtu. Menhit was a lion-headed war goddess, close in aspect to angry Sekhmet. But she walked on two legs and radiated hot light. She gave off a white aura, like

Family and Home

Families in ancient Egypt consisted of father, mother, children. The law protected the rights of women, allowing them to inherit, own, and cede property. Judging from artwork, we believe children were played with and tenderly loved. Many men, including pharaohs, had more than one wife, with all wives and children living in the same home, all equally valued by the law and all interacting lovingly.

An Egyptian painting showing parents receiving offerings from their sons

MENHIT

KHNUM

NIT

HEKET

NEBTU

KHNUM (CHNOUMIS)

marl pottery. Nebtu, in contrast, was the goddess of a nearby desert oasis—the watery counterpart to Menhit. She dressed in red, like silt pottery. It was as though Khnum had created these two wives from the same clay he used to create people. Being around them made him relish his accomplishments.

So Khnum was pretty busy, keeping all these wives happy. He declared himself the god of masculine fertility and called himself Min. He had a ram's strength and energy. He appeared as a ram, or as a man with a ram head or ram horns. Whatever his form, he was always ready to please his wives.

Still, Nit was in many ways his most important wife. The two were almost male and female aspects of a single deity. Like Nit, Khnum was there at the very beginning, and, like Nit, Khnum was an aspect of many gods. Through work with Satet, he was a Nile god, like Usir. Through work with Heket, he was an air god, like Shu. And because he was a potter, he created life, like Ra. In fact, when Ra created all matter, many believed he did it in the form of Khnum.

Khnum was a greedy god, with many wives: Here we see the hot lioness Menhit, the red-dressed but cool Nebtu, the frog goddess of birth Heket, and our weaving goddess Nit.

They spoke of Khnum-Ra. Perhaps it was Khnum-Ra who wept with joy that day long ago when his lost children Shu and Tefnut finally returned. Perhaps the teardrops of Khnum-Ra mixed with clay to form those first humans. Maybe Khnum's story and Ra's story are one.

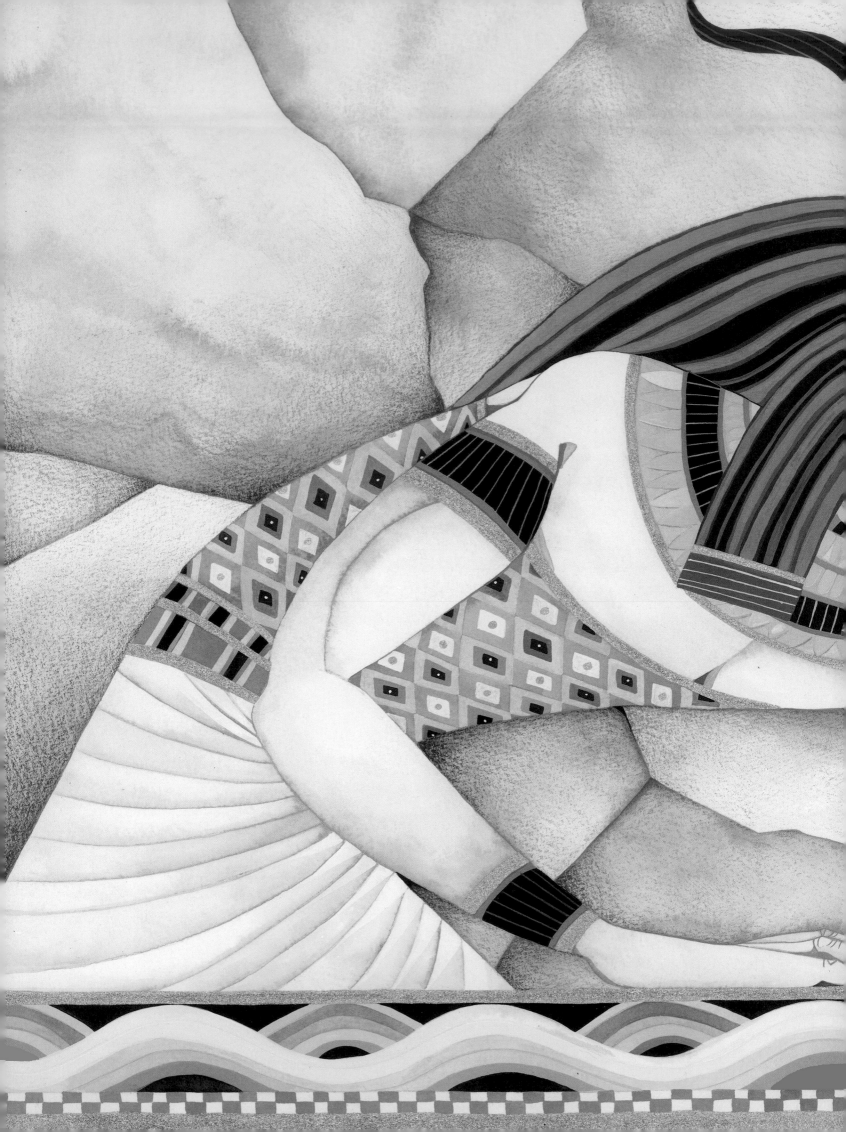

HGTV Magazine

92

SOBEK (SOUCHOS)
Crocodile God

When it came to eating, the gods and goddesses were a frugal and, actually, rather boring bunch. People sometimes made them elaborate food offerings: piles of dates, amphoras of wine, platters and platters of grilled vegetables, baked geese, stewed river fish, and vast arrays of sweets. But all that was folly. Deities preferred to eat simply; bread and fresh water generally did the trick.

Few liked vegetables and those who participated in rituals of the underworld Duat even hated onions. Some delighted in honey, while others found it bitter. The same was true of beer and wine. The goddess Hut Heru was known to be liberal in this regard, and she encouraged people to drink as they came to pray to her, to loosen their inhibitions so they could talk more freely and dance more joyously. The god Set had a reputation for getting drunk and bawdy just for the pleasure of it. The god Heru Wer drank to give himself courage in battle.

And all of them ate things people never thought of serving them, for they were beyond human consumption, such as precious stones. They consumed a daily portion of Ma'at—the spirit of order in the cosmos. Indeed, Ma'at was their essential food. And sometimes they drank their own tears and sweat.

But no god or goddess enjoyed eating flesh. If they indulged in meat at all, it was in moderation, without salt and always roasted, with much grain on the side. In truth,

Variety of Foods

Poor people in ancient Egypt subsisted on whole grain bread and barley beer—good sources of nutrients. Onion was enjoyed for flavor. Others drank wine and ate appropriately to their livelihood: Fishermen ate river fish; hunters ate game; animal tenders ate sheep, goat, geese, pigeons; farmers ate figs, dates, pomegranates, grapes, lettuce, garlic, onions, leeks, radishes, chicory, melon, cucumbers. The rich ate everything. So why were the gods so strict about their diets? Who knows?

Pomegranates have been cultivated since ancient times and are still eaten today.

some of them had a great distaste for certain meats. Ra, for example, would never eat turtle meat, since he considered turtles powers of evil and, thus, his enemies. And many considered eating meat crude and brutal.

Except for the god Sobek. And that wasn't his fault. Sobek was a crocodile, and crocodiles love meat, preferably raw. He couldn't help himself; it was built into him just as much as was the fact that he had a tail and a huge jaw and feet with claws. It was there from the start.

The start was in the original waters. Well, of course—he was a crocodile, after all. The goddess Nit, who was an extension of the watery chaos Nun, gave birth to two aquatic sons: the serpentine demon Apep, who descended immediately to the underworld Duat to plague Ra each night as he made his trip across the lake toward dawn, and the crocodile Sobek. Unlike

SOBEK (SOUCHOS)

Sobek loved the taste of flesh, as any crocodile does, yet he controlled his instincts as he carried the four little sons of Heru Wer to safe ground.

his brother Apep, however, Sobek didn't leave his mother at birth. Instead, he clung to her, as a child is wont to do. And she cradled him, as a mother should. She loved him true, and he loved her. And so Sobek's nature was a balance between two nearly contradictory things, the insatiable need to devour flesh and the understanding of how love binds one to another.

Early in his life he won the confidence of the gods for an act of random kindness. The god Heru Wer had swum through the waters of Nun and a blue water lily thus arose, which bloomed and gave forth four sons: Hapi, Duamutef, Amset, and Qebehsenuef. The four juvenile gods were helpless, there in the middle of the deep water. Sobek circled them. He couldn't help noticing their pudgy little arms and legs, their tender bellies, their fresh blood. His mouth must have watered at the thought of their juicy organs. His nostrils must have flared. Yet he kept that powerful jaw shut and offered his back, transporting the boys to the safety of land. They were babes, after all, and

he had been a babe, a cuddled one—the date his mother loved to smell, the pomegranate she held against her cheek. Who knows? Perhaps it was in honor of Sobek that these four gods eventually assumed the job of guards for the containers that held the organs and entrails of the dead.

At other times, though, Sobek's lust for flesh made a fool of him. In the ancient world, there were many scuffles among the gods from the various nations. During one of those periods, Sobek came across a band of enemies in his wanderings. As he saw it, the situation was perfect: He could eat to his heart's content and vanquish Egypt's foes at the same time. He devoured them all, down to their bones and the very last drops of their blood. But he saved their heads, so he could show them to the other Egyptian gods and goddesses and bask in their praise. When Sobek returned home, the deities saw him coming, took one look at the bloody booty, and shouted in disgust, "No! Don't let him eat those heads! Give him bread, give him bread." Poor Sobek was chagrined.

It was his fate to be admonished for his very nature.

That time Sobek went without punishment for his bestial behavior. But another time, he was not so lucky. When the god Set slew his brother Usir and ripped him into 14 pieces, he scattered those pieces across lands and waters. Sobek, great god of the marsh that he was, naturally came across a piece. He eyed it floating there. Clearly, Usir was dead, so one little piece was of no further use to him. Who would care? The morsel tantalized him. So he ate it. Snip, snap, gone.

Aset gathered the 13 other pieces of Usir, but she couldn't find the last one. A serpent told Aset that a monster had eaten that part. But Sobek was no monster. He was just a crocodile, a hungry carnivore for sure—but well-intentioned. What maliciousness could there be in taking a single bite of an already dead god? The act was the result of voraciousness, not meanness.

But the gods and goddesses didn't see it Sobek's way.

> Sobek ate a floating piece from the corpse of Usir—an innocent act for a crocodile. But he was punished severely for it: The gods cut out his tongue.

They punished him by cutting out his tongue. Even today crocodiles' tongues are stunted, so that few see them unless a croc opens his jaws especially wide.

Sobek later gave rides through the swamps to the boy Heru Sa Aset, son of Aset and Usir. Perhaps this was one way of atoning for eating part of the boy's father?

And even later, when the youth Heru Sa Aset had to fight the god Set for his father's throne, Sobek showed special kindness. Heru Sa Aset's mother Aset cut off his hands at one point in the struggle, for the gods and goddesses often let their rages and passions get the best of them. She threw them in the waters. The god Ra sent Sobek to retrieve them. Sobek searched and searched, confounded by the tricks of the river currents. Then he got the idea to build a trap, and soon he returned the severed hands to Heru Sa Aset.

Fishermen everywhere looked at that trap and made their own and thrived. Sobek became their patron god. And since he was lord of the marsh and the most fierce creature of the Nile, the source of all agricultural fecundity, Sobek was seen as a god of fertility, too. And, for no discernible reason, Sobek became the god to restore the sense of sight to the dead.

All in all, he was feared, meat-eater that he was. All in all, he was loved, beneficent god that he was.

SOBEK (SOUCHOS)

Cat Goddess

BASTET (BAST)
Cat Goddess

The cosmos was full of animals. But some were better than others.

The bull. Ah, the ancient auroch bull. They originated in India and over the millennia galloped across to northern Africa and Europe. They were enormous, taller than a man at the withers. Their lyre-shaped horns angled forward, perfect for tossing away an attacker. Or impaling him.

The cows and calves were red, but the bulls were kohl-black with a pale-eel spinal stripe that lent a majestic air, marking them as the most lethal of beasts. Not even a lion pride would take on an auroch bull. Hunting them took great courage or stupidity. Domesticating them took smarts and patience.

It made sense then that the gods Ra and Ptah transformed themselves at will into bulls and snorted and pawed the earth to remind everyone of their power. The ability of transformation was a lovely thing indeed.

When it came down to the basics, all deities had similar bodies, really; all were made of precious stones. The bones were silver; the flesh, gold; the hair, lapis lazuli. But divine beings could assume other colors because of associations. Usir's skin was black-green, to remind people of the rich, fertile soil left behind after the Nile's floods receded. Ra's skin was blue when he felt victorious and took on the name Amun-Ra and let swirls of air shoot up from his hands and head, all so that people would think of the destructive powers of wild winds.

Many carried the same objects—a *was*-scepter in one hand, with a forked bottom designed to catch serpents, and an ankh in the other, the cross with a loop on top. A few carried objects unique to them, though, such as the scribal palette of Tehuti, or objects that showed their nature, such as bow and arrows or a mace in the hand of the goddess Nit or the war god Montu.

Yet, the gods didn't all present themselves the same way to humans. The deities' ability to transform meant sometimes people didn't realize they were in the presence of a deity until something miraculous occurred.

Some deities refrained from transforming, and walked in human form only. Most older deities were like that—Shu and Nut and Geb. Geb often carried a goose on his head, but he didn't become a goose. Even Nebet Hut and Aset, the

A bronze and gold statue of the Goddess Bastet

Animal Worship

Many ancient cultures worshipped animals; some scholars believe that's Egypt's influence. Still, Egypt was special in worshipping so many animals. Scholars often say the reason for such worship is fear. Perhaps by praying to crocodiles, hippopotami, lions, serpents, people would be spared danger from those animals. But why a cat or frog? Maybe Bastet fended off disease because cats are good at catching vermin. And perhaps frogs ensured plentiful sweet water, since most frogs live in it.

SET

NEKHBET

TEHUTI

An assembly of the gods made quite a vision of sleek and scary animals and humans. But the kitty Bastet stood out as always approachable, useful, and, harmless. What a relief.

daughters of Geb and Nut, appeared only in human form, although sometimes Aset donned bird wings.

Other deities appeared in animal form only. The goddess Heket, the wife of Khnum, was a frog. The city of Ineb-Hedj worshipped a bull god called Hapu, the herald of the god Ptah. Lower Egypt worshipped the serpent goddess Wadjet.

Some deities appeared in mixed-animal form. The goddess Taweret had the torso and head of a hippopotamus, but lion limbs, and sometimes her tail was crocodilian while other times she carried a crocodile on her back.

But many gods appeared in multiple forms. The god Sobek was a man with a crocodile head or, instead, fully crocodile. The god Set could appear as a fabulous creature, with squared-off ears, a curved snout, a forked tail, and a canine body. He

BASTET (BAST)

HUT HERU

MAFTET

BASTET

seemed a blend of aardvark, jackal, and donkey. But sometimes
he was a man with only the head of this amazing animal.
Upper Egypt worshipped the goddess Nekhbet, who could be
fully woman, fully vulture, or a woman with a vulture head.

The ability of the deities to appear in different forms
helped distinguish among them. Tehuti, for example, was the
only god that appeared as an ibis or with an ibis head.

A god's appearance reflected his temperament of the
moment. Hut Heru could go as a woman with a cow head,
nurturing and milky, except when the goddess Sekhmet
within her burst forth as a woman with a lion head, or fully
lioness. We find the heads or bodies of rams and falcons and
vultures and cows and serpents and so many animals all
hosting deities, depending on their moods.

BASTET (BAST)

GEB

TEFNUT

SHU

NUT

Gods appeared in many forms: human, animal, a hybrid of both. Sometimes they were even a mix of several forms. Imagine looking at a frog and wondering, "Is she Heket?"

But only one goddess was a cat: Bastet. Many went as lions, revered out of fear. But the cat was appreciated out of admiration and affection. Farmers loved cats because they protected grain stores from rodents and snakes. Especially cobras. Oh, mongooses could kill cobras, too, so Maftet, the mongoose goddess, was sometimes mistaken for a cat. But it was only Bastet who purred.

City people, too, encouraged cats to come around. Cats kept the streets free of vermin, after all. And there was a mystery to the cat, the way it stayed aloof at times, yet could be endearingly friendly at others—this behavior made the cat prized. Besides, cats loved to bask in the all-powerful sun; they clearly understood the cosmos.

Rich people hung gold jewelry from the neck of their cats and fed them from their plates—bread, milk, fish slices. When

BASTET (BAST)

HEKET

HAPU

TAWERET

SOBEK

a cat died, the owners shaved their eyebrows in mourning and embalmed the cat with spices and drugs and mummified it in white linen, to preserve it for the everlasting. The penalty for killing a cat, even by accident, was death. Priests had cats roam temples to remind people of the goddess Bastet. When the city of Per-Bast, in the Nile delta, became a residence for the pharaoh, a temple to Bastet was built. It was smaller than some, but more beautiful than all others, with a canal around it and groves of fruit trees. Thousands of people made the annual pilgrimage to Per-Bast in April and May to gaze in awe at the massive statue of Bastet. Women shook sistrum rattles and men blew pipes and beat drums and played tambourines. People clapped and sang and danced in the streets, which ran with wine.

All this for Bastet—just a kitty. But a loved kitty is worth a dozen feared lions.

BASTET (BAST)

FUNERAL RITES
The Importance of Preparation and Judgment

Human beings had a body, which cast a shadow and was named at birth. But ancient Egyptians believed that at birth, the Ka came into existence, too. The Ka was a replica of the body, but without physical form. Humans also had the Ba. The Ba encompassed the personal power of an individual, almost like a personality, spiritual in nature.

The name of a person was important in life (witness how Aset gained Ra's powers by learning his secret name) and after death. The living needed to remember a deceased person's name for that person to prosper in the afterlife. So names were inscribed outside tombs. Inside tombs, names were on coffins. Inside coffins, names were on personal items. Often statues or carvings or paintings of the person would be at the tomb with the name displayed.

At death, the Ka and Ba separated from the body, but they needed to be reunited with it quickly, because it was their physical abode. The Ka, being the body's double, also needed to be fed. People put food in tombs for the Ka to eat, and in this way to nourish the corpse, the Ka's home. The Ba shared that home, but it was free to move around unrestricted, as a different mode for the individual to continue existing. It empowered the dead to leave the tomb and travel in a spiritual sense, so long as they returned to the body each night.

SATET

INPU

Satet washed each corpse, then Inpu put most of the organs in the four canopic jars. The corpses were wrapped in Nit's linen. Their bodies were now properly ready for judgment.

When people died, therefore, it was critical that their corpse be preserved properly. Without that, the afterlife was unattainable. So a funeral ritual developed.

The goddess Satet, wife of Khnum, washed the corpse with water from the Nile's source, purifying it.

Then Inpu took over. He taught humans to discard the brains of the dead, then put their organs into jars—canopic jars. He chose helpers—those four sons of Heru Wer who appeared in a blue water lily in the original waters of Nun, the babies the crocodile god Sobek carried safely to land. They were grown now, but without jurisdiction. Inpu loved them because his beloved aunt Aset favored the blue water lily. Inpu put the human-headed god of the south, Amset, in charge of the liver jar; the baboon-headed god of the north, Hapi, in charge of the lungs jar; the jackal-headed god of the east, Duamutef, in charge of the stomach jar; and the falcon-headed god of the west, Qebehsenuef, in charge of the intestines jar. Each sat on top of his jar and guarded the contents, which the deceased would need if welcomed into Duat.

NIT

Nit supplied white linen for mummification. Inpu taught people to desiccate the body and wrap it in these swaths to preserve it, a natural habit in this land of dry winds over desert sands, winds that sucked a corpse dry.

But bones and blood and organs weren't the only concern. When humans died, they lost voice. No one understood the power of voice better than Aset. Through the might of voice she brought her dead husband Usir back to life. Through the magic of words she stole the right to rule on earth from Ra. So Aset whispered sacred words to the temple priests to open dead men's mouths so they could speak in the ever-after. She hovered, making sure the priests performed the ceremony properly, then she accompanied the dead to Duat.

Hut Heru stood in the rare shade of an even rarer sycamore tree and gave water to the weary travelers as they reached Duat, or, if they preferred, the milky juice of the sycamore fig. In these moments, she felt her debt to Mehet-Weret, the "great cow" tide. She often wore a cow head as she served the dead.

The funeral boat carried the corpse to Tehuti and Usir, who extracted the heart and weighed it against a feather. A light heart meant a happy afterlife. A heavy one meant being devoured by Ammit.

Nebet Hut rode in the funeral boat with the dead, too. But her most important role was comforting their families. She knew how to cry piercingly, mournfully, like the screams of the black kite, for she mourned the loss of a loving husband. She taught families to grieve properly and at length, but then to release lamentations and swell their lungs with clean air and move on to appreciate the life ahead.

Heru Sa Aset joined in the procession, accompanying the dead to their point of judgment. Beside him, of course, was Inpu.

Once in Duat, the dead were looked over by Tehuti and Usir, as well as the four brother gods birthed in the blue water lily. So there they all were: Usir, Aset, Heru Sa Aset, Nebet Hut, Inpu. A family reunion—though the intricacies of it were known only to Nebet Hut.

Inpu was careful to keep each dead person's heart in the body until this point. The heart was the most important organ, the center of intellect, memory, and morality. Inpu tested it along the journey into Duat for how much it knew about the deities and how faithful it was. Now he took it out

AMMIT

and put it on scales to weigh against an ostrich feather.

What's in an ostrich feather? The balance of the cosmos, divine order. The rising and setting of the sun. The flooding and ebbing of the Nile. The patterns of the stars. Each person was held responsible for preserving this order, Ma'at, for if he didn't, chaos would ensue. The feather itself was the hieroglyph for Ma'at's name.

If a person had not committed crimes that disordered the natural order, his or her heart would be as light as the feather. If not, the heart would sink.

Usir judged the balances. He was true to his vows; as long as people had striven to lead a reasonably balanced life, Usir accepted them into the underworld, and their Ba could be seen by friends and family as stars in the skies.

But a heavy heart condemned its owner to a second death, which Tehuti recorded. Evil hearts were thrown to Ammit, a creature part crocodile, part hippo, part lion—the embodiment of divine retribution. Ammit rose from a lake of fire and devoured them.

IMHOTEP (IMUTHES)

God of Medicine and Architecture

Humans died. Deities could die, too; Set had proved that when he killed his brother Usir. But humans died regularly—it was in their nature. Still, if people behaved well in life, then when they died, they had a chance at eternal life, so long as their body was cared for according to precise rules, including mummification and proper burial. Rich people had special tombs built, called mastabas. They were filled with ample provisions, so that the deceased would not go hungry.

The pharaoh, the chief ruler of all Egypt, had the greatest stake in making sure his body was cared for, since after death he would merge with a god—and live on forever with all the powers a god had. The goddess Heket, one of the wives of Khnum, helped pharaohs after death by showing them the way up to the sky.

And so the pharaohs began building tombs that befit a god. Their mastabas were underground with a maze of tunnels leading to a central granite-lined chamber to hold the deceased's body. Off this room were galleries with storerooms, all of them beautifully decorated with glazed blue tiles. The facades of the mastabas were made of brick and mud. The pharaohs erected tall stelae—great pointed columns—outside their tombs, with suitable carvings, typically falcons. These lofty structures, these suitable tombs, were the residence of the pharaoh after death.

Ancient Medicine

Medicine in ancient Egypt related to religion and magic, because physicians were priests. Nevertheless, physicians did not rely solely on incantations and spells. They searched the natural world for sources of medicine: lizard flesh, bat blood, crocodile dung, ear wax, lion fat. Ancient Egyptians are the fore-runners of organo-therapy. Physicians also used plant extracts for drugs, including castor oil, copper salts, and calamus. They stumbled on important remedies, such as honey as an antibiotic on wounds.

Honey was an important medicine in ancient times.

Imhotep was a well-educated man living during the Third Dynasty. He studied continually and gathered scribes around him and they talked of the nature of the cosmos and of the workings of the natural world. Imhotep knew much about the architecture of humans—the way the body worked. He was a physician and he extracted fluids from plants to make medicines. He pulled rotting teeth and he did surgeries on ailing organs. He taught others about how the blood circulated through the body and what each organ was responsible for. Imhotep also knew much about the architecture of human-made objects: tools and furniture and buildings. He taught about these things, too. Soon he gained a reputation as a wise man and became a high priest in the city of Iunu.

This was a difficult time for Egypt. Seven years passed without the Nile River rising and overflowing its banks. The farmers grew

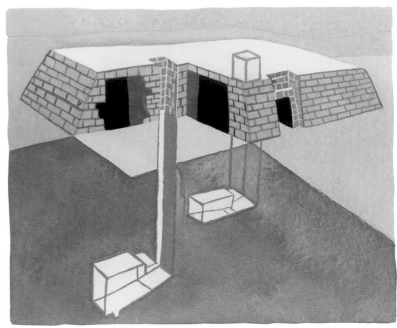

The bricks for these mastabas came from Nile River mud, baked in the sun. The scenes painted on interior walls showed typical pastimes, often the favorite ones of the deceased.

desperate, for without that flooding the soil became infertile. Seeds dried up before they could even be planted. Many that did begin to grow failed for lack of nutrients and water. Harvests were meager. Old people were reduced to sitting against walls, moving as little as possible. Children cried. Young adults staggered with hunger, trying to carry on. Never was the vulnerability and fragility of life more starkly evident.

In his devotion, the scholar priest Imhotep thought about the mastabas. He thought about the passing of time, the effects of winds and rains. And he worried. The brick and mud of the mastabas were hardened by the flaming Egyptian sun, but brick and mud are simply brick and mud. They crumble eventually. What good was a pharaoh's tomb that wouldn't last forever?

So Imhotep counseled the Pharaoh Netjerikhet, more commonly known as Djoser, to build a new type of tomb,

Djoser's step pyramid was the tallest building of its time. A wall 30 feet (9 m) high enclosed the pyramid, as well as grounds as large as a town, with temples and courtyards.

made of mastabas stacked on top of one another, each one a little smaller than the one below it, so that they rose up in steps. The trick to it all was that the building blocks would be stone. After all, limestone was abundant in Lower Egypt, especially near the coast. It would be possible to quarry limestone close by the capital of Ineb-Hedj and build the stone tomb—the step pyramid—in the necropolis (the cemetery of tombs) in nearby Saqqara. And limestone was white; when polished it would catch the glint of the sun and thus people would be able to see the glory of the towering pyramid from far away. Besides, a stone pyramid would honor the gods, and maybe they would end this hideous famine.

It was a revolutionary idea. How could one build a huge pyramid from heavy stone? What would keep it from crashing through simply because of the weight? Imhotep began with a

normal mastaba—a granite-lined chamber surrounded
by rooms of brick and mud. He encased that inside
a four-stepped pyramid, each layer of limestone, then
finally heightened it to six steps. Indeed, people
traveling to the capital city could see the pyramid when
they were still several days' travel away.

The taller these step pyramids grew, the more they
seemed like stairs leading to the heavens. The various family
lines of pharaohs, the dynasties, felt confident of a royal hereafter. And these step pyramids paved the way for the smooth-
sided pyramids that the whole world became familiar with.

The feat of building the step pyramids was so remarkable
that Imhotep's name became sacred throughout the land, and
nearly 2,000 years later he was recognized as a god, the god
of medicine and architecture. In so many ways Imhotep
embodied the best of ancient Egypt's sensibilities: interest
in the divine combined with attention to the needs of body,
mind, and spirit on earth.

IMHOTEP (IMUTHES)

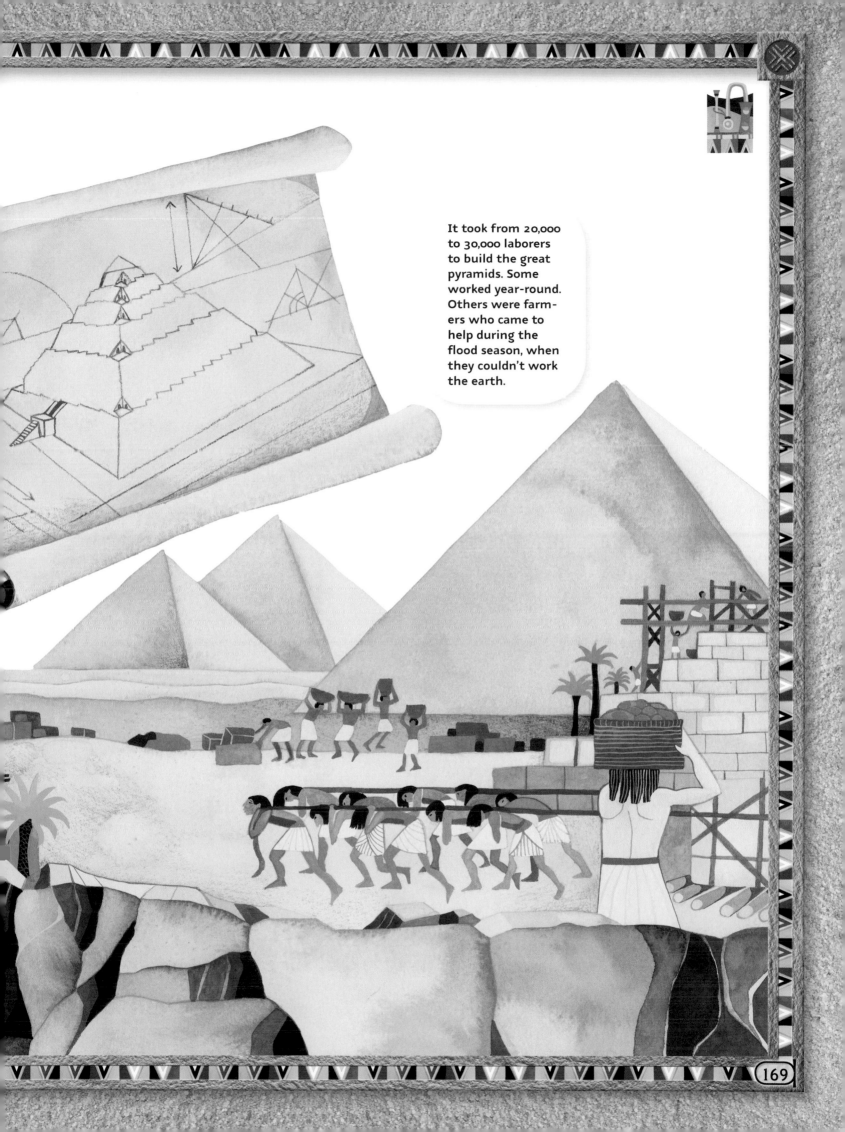

It took from 20,000 to 30,000 laborers to build the great pyramids. Some worked year-round. Others were farmers who came to help during the flood season, when they couldn't work the earth.

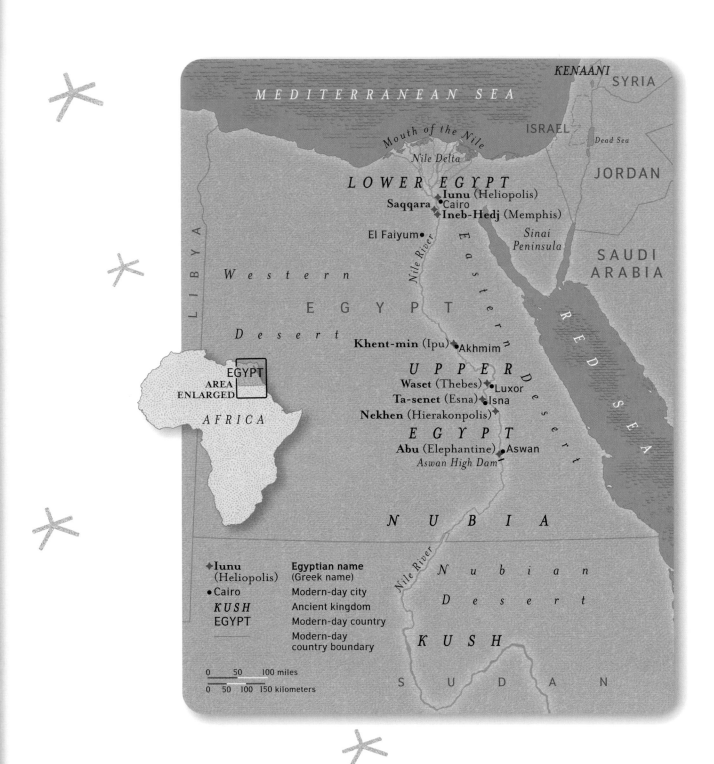

KENAANI
SYRIA

MEDITERRANEAN SEA

ISRAEL

Dead Sea

JORDAN

Mouth of the Nile

Nile Delta

LOWER EGYPT

◆**Iunu** (Heliopolis)

Saqqara ◆ • Cairo

◆ **Ineb-Hedj** (Memphis)

El Faiyum •

Nile River

Sinai
Peninsula

Eastern

SAUDI
ARABIA

LIBYA

Western

RED SEA

E G Y P T

D e s e r t

Khent-min (Ipu) • Akhmim

U P P E R

Waset (Thebes) ◆ • Luxor

Ta-senet (Esna) ◆ • Isna

Nekhen (Hierakonpolis) ◆

Desert

EGYPT

AREA
ENLARGED

AFRICA

E G Y P T

Abu (Elephantine) ◆ • Aswan

Aswan High Dam

N U B I A

N u b i a n

D e s e r t

Nile River

◆**Iunu**
(Heliopolis)   **Egyptian name**
               (Greek name)

• Cairo   Modern-day city

KUSH   Ancient kingdom

EGYPT   Modern-day country

——   Modern-day
                country boundary

K U S H

0   50   100 miles

0   50   100 150 kilometers

S U D A N

SUDAN

TIME LINE OF ANCIENT EGYPT

THROUGH THE FINAL DYNASTY

circa 7000 B.C.
The earliest settlers came to the Nile valley.

7000 B.C.–3900 B.C.
Many villages arose in the Nile delta. People hunted, fished, and practiced agriculture. Housing consisted of mud huts.
Pottery had decorative illustrations or geometric patterns, and often was painted, first with white and later with reds.

3900 B.C.–3050 B.C.
People developed papyrus scrolls, metal tools and weapons, and gold, silver, and copper jewelry. Linen was developed (the first
record of linen sails for boats is circa 3200 B.C.). Many local deities were worshipped, most having animal heads and human bodies.

3050 B.C.–2950 B.C.
Archaic Period (Dynasty 0*):
Village kings banded together into Upper Egypt and Lower Egypt. Local deities were replaced by the universal gods
of the Great Pesedjet. Many stone vessels from this time have been preserved. (*The "zero" dynasty was discovered later, after the
others had already been numbered, hence it was simply tacked on as zero.)

2950 B.C.–2575 B.C.
Early Dynastic Period (1st through 3rd Dynasties):
Domestic and foreign trade flourished. Upper and Lower Egypt unified under the Pharaoh Den in 2880 B.C.

2575 B.C.–2125 B.C.
Old Kingdom (4th through 8th Dynasties):
The time of the pyramids. The great pyramids were constructed circa 2500 B.C.

2125 B.C.–2010 B.C.
1st Intermediate Period (9th through 11th Dynasties):
This era was riddled with civil war in the region.

2010 B.C.–1630 B.C.
Middle Kingdom (12th and 13th Dynasties):
Another period of unification. Circa 1800 B.C. the Hyksos people of western Asia began moving into the
eastern Nile delta. The Hyksos brought new crops and new breeds of domesticated animals, and introduced the horse
and chariot. They took power at the end of the 13th Dynasty, which would result in the 2nd Intermediate Period.

1630 B.C.–1539 B.C.
2nd Intermediate Period (14th through 17th Dynasties):
Another period of civil war.

1539 B.C.–1069 B.C.
New Kingdom (18th through 20th Dynasties):
A period of unification, during which Nubia, to the south, was taken over.

1069 B.C.–664 B.C.
3rd Intermediate Period (21st through 25th Dynasties):
A period of internal conflict and invasions. The Libyans from the northwest took control during the 22nd Dynasty. The Kushites
from the west then invaded, and gained power from the Libyans. The Assyrians from Mesopotamia invaded multiple times, and
finally brought down the 25th Dynasty.

664 B.C.–332 B.C.
Late Period (26th through 31st Dynasties):
Egypt reunified under Assyrian rule and fought off the Babylonians. The Persians invaded once,
and then again, remaining for the last 11 years.

CAST OF CHARACTERS

Egyptian Name: ASET

Greek Name: Isis

Title: Woman of the Lotus and Devoted Wife and Mother

Symbol: headdress shaped like a throne, sun disk with cow horns, sycamore tree

Source: Daughter of Geb and Nut

Married to: Usir

Egyptian Name: GEB

Greek Name: Kronos

Title: God of the Earth

Symbol: goose, plants, phallus

Source: Son of Shu and Tefnut

Married to: Nut

Egyptian Name: BASTET

Greek Name: Bast

Title: Cat Goddess

Symbol: cat; lioness; sistrum, a percussion instrument

Source: (perhaps) Daughter of Ra and Aset

Married to: that form of Ra known as Ptah

Egyptian Name: HERU SA ASET

Greek Name: Horus the Younger

Title: Young Warrior God and King

Symbol: the Wadjet eye, with an eyebrow above and a teardrop and curling strand below

Source: Son of Aset and Usir

Married to: (perhaps) the scorpion goddess Ta-Bitjet

Egyptian Name: HERU WER

Greek Name: Horus the Elder

Title: Winged Sun Disk and Protector of Egypt

Symbol: winged sun disk

Source: Son of Geb and Nut

Married to: (perhaps) the scorpion goddess Ta-Bitjet

Egyptian Name: HUT HERU

Greek Name: Hathor

Title: Goddess of Delights

Symbol: the sistrum, a percussion instrument

Source: Ra's eye

Married to: (perhaps) Ra

Egyptian Name: KHNUM

Greek Name: Chnoumis

Title: God of the Potter's Wheel

Symbol: the potter's wheel

Source: Khnum was there at the very beginning; perhaps he is an aspect of Ra.

Married to: Nit, Satet, Heket, Menhit, Nebtu

Egyptian Name: IMHOTEP

Greek Name: Imuthes

Title: God of Medicine and Architecture

Symbol: scrolls about medicine and architecture

Source: He was born human, son of Kheredu-ankh (mother) and Kanofer (father), in the town of Ineb Hedj.

Married to: Ronfrenofert

Egyptian Name: NEBET HUT

Greek Name: Nephthys

Title: Goddess of Service

Symbol: mummy cloth, the home

Source: Daughter of Geb and Nut

Married to: Set

Egyptian Name: INPU

Greek Name: Anubis

Title: God of Mummification

Symbol: the flail; the *imiut* fetish, which was a stuffed, headless animal skin, tied by the tail to a pole

Source: Son of Nebet Hut and Usir or, perhaps, Ra

Married to: Anput

continued from page 173

Egyptian Name: NIT

Greek Name: Neith

Title: Warrior Goddess and Weaver of the Cosmos

Symbol: the bow, the shield, the crossed arrows

Source: Nit rose spontaneously from the vast wetness called Nun, just like Ra. She is the first goddess (unless one calls Nun a goddess).

Married to: Khnum

Egyptian Name: RA

Greek Name: Helios

Title: God of Radiance

Symbol: solar disk with serpent coiled around it

Source: Ra rose spontaneously from the vast wetness called Nun. He is the first god.

Married to: Ra's spirit merged with everything and anything.

Egyptian Name: NUT

Greek Name: Neuth

Title: Goddess of the Sky

Symbol: sky, star

Source: Daughter of Shu and Tefnut

Married to: Geb

Egyptian Name: SEKHMET

Greek Name: Sachmis

Title: Goddess of Vengeance

Symbol: sun disk, linen the color of blood

Source: The anger of Hut Heru

Married to: that form of Ra known as Ptah

Egyptian Name: SET

Greek Name: Seth

Title: Envious God

Symbol: the was-scepter, with a forked end and an animal head at the top

Source: Son of Geb and Nut

Married to: Nebet Hut

Egyptian Name: SHU

Greek Name: Shu

Title: God of Wind and Air

Symbol: ostrich feather

Source: Ra's breath

Married to: Tefnut

Egyptian Name: TEHUTI

Greek Name: Thoth

Title: God of Knowledge

Symbol: papyrus scroll, crescent moon

Source: Ra's tongue

Married to: Seshat and, in a sense, Ma'at

Egyptian Name: SOBEK

Greek Name: Souchos

Title: Crocodile God

Symbol: crocodile

Source: Son of Nit

Married to: the snake goddess Renenutet

Egyptian Name: USIR

Greek Name: Osiris

Title: God of the Afterlife

Symbol: crook and flail

Source: Son of Geb and Nut

Married to: Aset

Egyptian Name: TEFNUT

Greek Name: Tphenis

Title: Goddess of Moisture

Symbol: lioness

Source: Ra's spit

Married to: Shu

How many deities did the Egyptians worship? And what were their stories? The answers to these questions are not simple. Prehistoric communities were active in Egypt during the Paleolithic Period (the Stone Age), gathering plants and scavenging animals. By around 5400 B.C. Neolithic cultures had formed in the Nile valley, consisting of several agricultural villages and nomadic necropolises. At some point Lower Egypt (including the delta area) and Upper Egypt (all the way to the cataracts of the Nile) became a cohesive country. That is, they united culturally and, eventually, politically. Books give different precise dates for the various periods of the country's history, where these differences can be as much as centuries and where the number of dynasties is recorded to be fewer or more. One approximation of ancient Egypt is given in the Time Line (see page 171), which covers our earliest information about human habitation in Egypt through the final dynasty, which ended in 332 B.C.

The Macedonian Period followed, from 332 to 305 B.C. During this time Alexander the Great of Macedon conquered the Persian empire, and captured Egypt along with it. The rule of the Macedonian dynasty ended when Ptolemy, one of Alexander's generals and the governor of Egypt, declared himself an independent king, thus founding the Ptolemaic dynasty—the last line of independent pharaohs of Egypt (albeit of foreign origin). The Ptolemaic Period ran until 30 B.C.; Macedonian and Greek immigrants ruled Egypt in this time of great unrest, during which the Romans intervened in conflicts between members of the Ptolemaic dynasty. The Romans made Egypt an Imperial province (30 B.C.–A.D. 395), and then the Byzantines ruled (395–640).

This bronze coin shows a profile. It might be Ptolemy IV, the fourth Greek ruler of Egypt; or it might be Alexander the Great, who ruled lands around the Mediterranean Sea from Greece through Egypt.

Over the nearly 5,000 years before the Greeks took over, we have few authoritative and extensive texts telling us about the deities, unlike the situation in ancient Greece, where we have individual poets (Hesiod, Homer, Apollodorus, and others—but they were quite late, dating from around 800 B.C. and later) whose writings have survived through the ages. Instead, from Egypt we rely on scattered papyrus books (scrolls), usually only partial, and inscriptions in temples and tombs.

Writing began in Egypt very early; in fact, Egyptian tax records are among the earliest proto-writings we have yet discovered in the world. Proto-writing is rudimentary writing, consisting mostly of numbers and symbols used as mnemonic devices. It was employed in record-keeping centuries before people used actual script for representing the utterances of language. The oldest true writing we know of goes back to around 3200 B.C., in Sumer. Egypt also shows true writing around then, perhaps influenced by Sumer. In tombs of officials from as early as the Third Dynasty we find continuous texts, mostly royal edicts. Soon stories about the deities appeared, though abbreviated. Some famous ones are called the Pyramid texts; they are composite works written by several scribes over many years, starting in the Old Kingdom (Fifth Dynasty, found in the

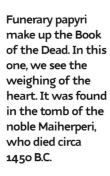

Funerary papyri make up the Book of the Dead. In this one, we see the weighing of the heart. It was found in the tomb of the noble Maiherperi, who died circa 1450 B.C.

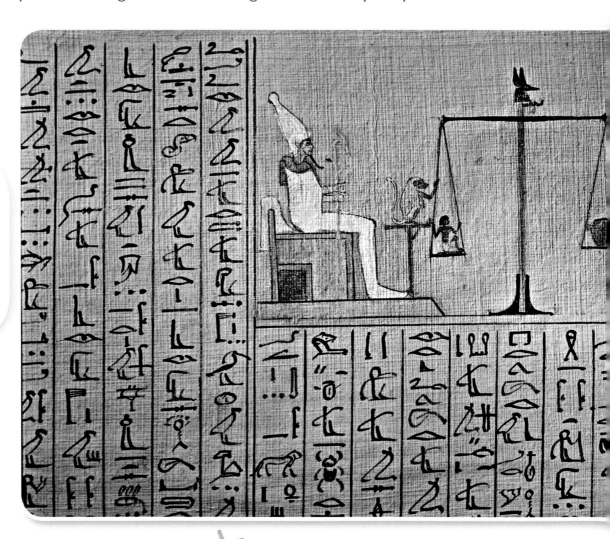

tomb of Pharaoh Unas). From the Pyramid texts it would appear that as new ideas about the deities arose, they did not supplant old ones, but, rather, coexisted with them, as though the contradictions didn't matter. By the time of the Middle Kingdom a full-fledged literature had developed. A famous text from the New Kingdom is known as the Book of the Dead, and it tells us about funerary rituals.

Like the Pyramid texts, it is a composite work, sometimes internally inconsistent. The New Kingdom also spawned hymns to various gods.

Additional information about the deities comes from hymns and religious inscriptions carved in hieroglyphics on ancient walls, from statues and drawings of them, from temples built in their honor. All these taken together would suggest the ancient Egyptians worshipped hundreds of deities, at the least.

Yet, unlike the gods and goddesses of ancient Greece or Rome, the Egyptian gods and goddesses were not easily distinguishable, one from another. Many gods were hailed as the creator of everything and everyone. Many goddesses were prayed to for help in childbirth. Often deities seemed to be flip sides of the same coin. For example, both Ra and Usir ruled over eternal matters; Ra is associated with the passage of the sun from sunrise to sunset, when it appears to die, but then reappears, as though reborn, the next dawn, while Usir is associated with the infinite everlasting state that follows life on earth. They complement each other in that one rules the life of light, the other rules the life of dark—one rules above the firmament and one rules below it. Only together do we see a complete sovereignty.

So how on earth does one make a definitive list of these slippery, entangled deities?

The people of ancient Egypt were spread out over a vast distance, and even though the Nile connected them, most people didn't travel far from their home. That may be why only a few deities were known at the national level. Instead, there were, eventually (that is, by the time of the New Kingdom), 42 administrative districts, each with multiple small villages, and each locality had at least one of its own gods. For example, Ptah played a similar role in the city Ineb Hedj (and, later on, nationally) to that played by Amun in the city of Waset, and to that played by Atum in the city of Iunu, and to that played by Khnum in the city of Ta-senet (he was called Min in his role as fertility god in the city of Khent-min), and to that played by Heru Wer in the city of Nekhen—and all of them overlapped with the national role of Ra. Sometimes these gods had a goddess partner and a child, so that they formed triads in their localities. Ptah, for example, formed a sacred triad with Sekhmet and Nefertem; Amun formed a sacred triad with Mut and Khonsu; and so on. Since the gods and goddesses were responsible for the very same set of natural phenomena (the rising and setting of the sun, the wind, the stars, the moon, rain, the flooding of the Nile River, fertility, survival through childbirth and child-hood, eventual death, and so on) and for the same set of values and skills (divine order, justice, agriculture, writing, weaving), viewed all together there were, quite naturally, many overlapping deities. Competing cities had competing accounts of the creation and of various stories about the deities as well as their own unique stories—and all of this changed over time, as always happens in human society.

Still, even within a local set of gods and goddesses, the tendency to have them share traits is strong. While there was a hierarchy among the deities, with some being older than others and some being generally more powerful or important than others, it is hard to find stories in which the Egyptian deities have clearly delineated personalities, except for a handful—

such as Set and Sobek and Aset. In fact, there aren't many stories about the deities, and most of the ones that we have today were written down not by the ancient Egyptians, but by the Greeks, who may well have embellished tales they heard from Egyptians, imposing their own views of numinous behavior. But if the ancient Egyptian gods and goddesses really weren't discrete, that would be a natural reason not to have multiple stories recounting their individual acts.

So perhaps the best approach is not to work so hard at teasing the Egyptian deities apart, but, instead, to view them as a gigantic whole, responsible for the cosmos in all its various predictable and unpredictable events, and thus having myriad parts that reflect that regularity and that capriciousness. With this view, the Egyptian religion might have been closer to monotheist ones than to polytheist ones.

In this book I have worked from the sources available to me, relying first on those written by Egyptians, but not eschewing those written by Greeks. Certain themes and images come up so often on the ancient walls and in the ancient statuary and

The largest ancient religious site in the world, the Temple at Karnak was built in the Middle Kingdom and was expanded many times over the centuries. Some of the columns are 69 feet (21 m) tall.

other artifacts that it would be remiss of me to fail to use them in this book, no matter who recorded the tales concerning them. For example, in Aset's chapter the part of the story that takes place in Kubna comes from a story by the Greek scholar Plutarch. So it might or might not be of Egyptian origin. But many likenesses of Aset show her holding the infant prince, so I wanted to present that to the reader.

Further, when I faced conflicting stories, I made choices on aesthetic grounds. For one, there are alternative accounts of the origin of people. Many involve tears. But in some there is a complication regarding the eyes of Ra. Did the first eye get replaced in her absence and then weep in rage? Was it instead the first eye that went wandering, and Ra sent Tefnut and Shu to bring her back and she cried in rebellion at being forced to return? I chose the present version because it may go back to early 3rd millennium B.C.—so it might be the oldest—and because it is more lovely to me.

For another, in some versions of the myths, Heru Sa Aset was already born before Set ripped Usir apart. But I chose the version with him born after Usir was killed, because it is more dramatic and more poignant, in my eyes.

Other times gaps in the myths left me with a patching job. For example, accounts of Inpu's origins vary widely in details, some conflicting and some simply missing. The one commonality is that Nebet Hut is his mother. I have kept this commonality and crafted an origin for him that slides into the other tales here well, I hope.

And, finally, some of the choices I made were nearly random. For example, some myths say the four gods who guarded the funerary canopic jars were the children of Ra, not Heru Wer. But there's much confusion and melding between Heru Wer and Ra generally, so the choice had no consequences I could see, and Heru Wer seems to be in the older account of this myth.

I exercised the liberty of adding details that rounded scenes out: for example, the rhythm leading to the beating heart of Ra in the creation myth and the presence of the hoopoe birds in the story of Aset going to Kubna.

My constant and sincere hope is to have presented stories with as genuine an ancient Egyptian sensibility as I could manage to glean from the many sources I consulted.

I thank Samir Abbass for guiding me in Egypt in 2010 and discussing with me not just inscriptions on temples and tombs, but the writings of the Greek historian Herodotus and variations between Egyptian and Greek versions of some myths. I thank Ian Moyer for giving comments on drafts, feeding me bibliographic sources, making both factual and creative suggestions, and generally being a wonderful and cheerful support. I thank the editorial and design staff at National Geographic for countless details, including Priyanka Lamichhane, David M. Seager, and Jennifer Emmett.

BIBLIOGRAPHY

The sources most often used are:

Allen, Thomas George. *The Book of the Dead or the Book of Going Forth by Day: Ideas of the Ancient Egyptians Concerning the Hereafter as Expressed in Their Own Terms.* Chicago: Chicago University Press, 1974.

Atiya, Farid S. *Ancient Egypt.* Giza, Egypt: Farid Atiya Press, 2006.

Baines, J. "Egyptian Myth and Discourse: Myth, Gods, and the Early Written and Iconographic Record." *Journal of Near Eastern Studies* 50 (1991): 81-105.

Budge, E. A. Wallis. *The Book of the Dead.* Garsington, UK: Benediction Books, 2010. First published in 1895 by the British Museum, London.

Budge, E. A. Wallis. *From Fetish to God in Ancient Egypt.* Kila, Mont.: Kessinger Publishing, LLC, 2010. First published in 1934 by Oxford University Press.

Budge, E. A. Wallis. *The Gods of the Egyptians,* Volumes 1 and 2. Mineola, N.Y.: Dover Publications, 1969. First published in 1904 by the Open Court Publishing Company, Chicago, and Methuen & Company, London.

Faulkner, Raymond O. *The Ancient Egyptian Coffin Texts.* Warminster: Aris and Phillips Ltd., 1973–1978.

Faulkner, Raymond O. *The Ancient Egyptian Pyramid Texts.* Oxford: Oxford University Press, 1969.

Goebs, Katja. "A Functional Approach to Egyptian Myths and Themes." *Journal of Ancient Near Eastern Religions* 2 (2002): 27-59.

Hart, George. *Egyptian Myths.* Austin: University of Texas Press, 1990. First published in London.

Hart, George. *The Routledge Dictionary of Egyptian Gods and Goddesses.* London and New York: Routledge, 2005.

Lichtheim, Miriam. *Ancient Egyptian Literature,* Volumes I-III. Berkeley: University of California Press, 1973–1980.

Pinch, Geraldine. *Egyptian Myth: A Very Short Introduction.* Oxford: Oxford University Press, 2004.

Pinch, Geraldine. *Egyptian Mythology: A Guide to the Gods, Goddesses, and Traditions of Ancient Egypt.* Oxford: Oxford University Press, 2002.

Pinch, Geraldine. *Handbook of Egyptian Mythology.* Santa Barbara: University of California Press, 2002.

Simpson, William Kelley, ed. *The Literature of Ancient Egypt: An Anthology of Stories, Instructions, Stelae, Autobiographies, and Poetry,* 3rd ed. New Haven, Conn.: Yale University Press, 2003.

Van Dijk, Jacobus. "Myth and Mythmaking in Ancient Egypt." In *Civilizations of the Ancient Near East,* Volume III, 1697–1709, edited by Jack M. Sasson. New York: Hendrickson Publishers, 1995.

Many other texts were consulted, both for overviews and for details, including:

Allen, James P. *Middle Egyptian: An Introduction to the Language and Culture of Hieroglyphs,* 2nd ed. Cambridge: Cambridge University Press, 2010.

Allen, Troy D. *The Ancient Egyptian Family: Kinship and Social Structure.* New York: Routledge, 2009.

Anderson, Kay, Mona Domosh, Steve Pile, and Nigel Thrift. *Handbook of Cultural Geography.* London: Sage Publications, 2003.

Asante, Molefi K. and Ama Mazama. *Encyclopedia of African Religion,* Volume 1. London: Sage Publications, 2008.

Boylan, Patrick. *Thoth, the Hermes of Egypt.* Oxford: Oxford University Press, 1922.

Breyer, Michelle. *Ancient Egypt.* Westminster, Calif.: Teacher Created Resources, 1996.

Crum, Walter E. *A Coptic Dictionary.* Oxford: Oxford University Press, 1939.

David, Rosalie. *Handbook to Life in Ancient Egypt,* revised edition. Oxford: Oxford University Press, 2007.

Drobnick, Jim, ed. *The Smell Culture Reader.* London: Berg Publishers, 2006.

Dunand, Françoise, Roger Lichtenberg, and David Lorton. *Mummies and Death in Egypt.* Ithaca, N.Y.: Cornell University Press, 2006.

Dunand, Françoise, and Christiane Zivie-Coche. *Gods and Men in Egypt: 3000 BCE to 395 CE.* Ithaca, N.Y.: Cornell University Press, 2004.

Frankfort, Henri. *Ancient Egyptian Religion: An Interpretation.* New York: Columbia University Press, 1961.

Garry, Jane, and Hasan M. El-Shamy, eds. *Archetypes and Motifs in Folklore and Literature: A Handbook.* Armonk, N.Y.: M. E. Sharpe Inc., 2005.

Grimal, Nicolás-Christophe. English translation. *A History of Ancient Egypt.* London: Blackwell, 1992.

Hornung, Erik. *History of Ancient Egypt: An Introduction.* Ithaca, N.Y.: Cornell University Press, 1999.

Kassing, Gayle. *History of Dance: An Interactive Arts Approach.* Champaign, Ill.: Human Kinetics, 2007.

Keene, John Harrington. *Fishing Tackle: Its Materials and Manufacture.* New York: Ward, Lock and Co. Made available in 2008 by Amazon's online publishing: CreateSpace. First published in 1886.

Kerr, Christine, and Janice Hoshino. *Family Art Therapy: Foundations of Theory and Practice.* New York: Routledge, 2007.

Layton, Bentley. *A Coptic Grammar.* Wiesbaden: Harrassowitz Verlag, 2000.

Lee, Raymond L. and Alistair B. Fraser. *The Rainbow Bridge: Rainbows in Art, Myth, and Science.* University Park: Pennsylvania State University Press, 2001.

Littleton, C. Scott. *Gods, Goddesses, and Mythology,* Volume 11. New York: Marshall Cavendish Corporation, 2005.

Lucas, Alfred. *Ancient Egyptian Materials and Industries,* 3rd ed. Timperly, Altrincham: The St. Ann's Press, 1948.

Maspero, Gaston, and A. H. Sayce. *History of Egypt,* Parts 1 and 2. Reprinted. Kila, Mont.: Kessinger Publishing, LLC, 2003.

Massey, Gerald. *Ancient Egypt: The Light of the World.* Sioux Falls, S. Dak.: NuVision Publications, LLC, 2008.

Meeks, Dimitri, and Christine Favard-Meeks. *Daily Life of the Egyptian Gods.* Ithaca, N.Y.: Cornell University Press, 1996.

Moore, George Foot. *History of Religions,* Volume 1. New York: Charles Scribner's Sons, 1922.

Muller, W. Max. *Egyptian Mythology.* Norwood, Mass.: The Plimpton Press, 1918.

Pinch, Geraldine. *Magic in Ancient Egypt.* Austin: University of Texas Press, 1995.

Potts, Albert M. *The World's Eye.* Lexington: The University Press of Kentucky, 1982.

Radcliffe, William. *Fishing From the Earliest Times.* Chicago Ridge: Ares Publishers, 1921.

Redmount, Carol A. "Ethnicity, Pottery, and the Hyksos at Tell El-Maskhuta in the Egyptian Delta." *Biblical Archaeologist* 58 (1995): 188.

Remler, Pat. *Egyptian Mythology A to Z.* New York: Infobase Publishing, 2000.

Renouf, P. Le Page. *The Origin and Growth of Religion as Illustrated by the Religion of Ancient Egypt.* New York: Charles Scribner's Sons, 1880.

Sayce, A. H. *The Religions of Ancient Egypt and Babylonia.* Edinburgh: T&T Clark, 1902.

Schomp, Virginia. *The Ancient Egyptians.* Tarrytown, N.Y.: Marshall Cavendish, 2007.

Shafer, Byron E., ed. *Religion in Ancient Egypt: Gods, Myths, and Personal Practice.* Ithaca, N.Y.: Cornell University Press, 1992.

Shorter, Alan W. *The Egyptian Gods: A Handbook.* London: Routledge & Kegan Paul, 1937.

Smith, William Stevenson, and William Kelly Simpson. *The Art and Architecture of Ancient Egypt.* New Haven, Conn.: Yale University Press, 1998.

Taylor, John. *Death and the Afterlife in Ancient Egypt.* Chicago: University of Chicago Press, 2001.

Traunecker, Claude. *The Gods of Egypt.* Ithaca, N.Y.: Cornell University Press, 2001.

Van De Mieroop, Marc. *A History of Ancient Egypt.* Oxford: Wiley-Blackwell, 2010.

Van Sertima, Ivan. *Black Women in Antiquity.* Piscataway, N.J.: Transaction Publishers, 1988.

Wilkinson, Toby A. H. *Lives of the Ancient Egyptians.* London: Thames & Hudson, 2007.

Wilkinson, Toby A. H. *The Rise and Fall of Ancient Egypt.* London: Bloomsbury Publishing, 2010.

FIND OUT MORE

BOOKS

Donoughue, Carol, *The Mystery of the Hieroglyphs*. Oxford University Press, 1999.
Hopping, Lorraine Jean, *Explore Within an Egyptian Mummy*. Silver Dolphin Books, 2008.
Longley, Elizabeth and John James, *Egyptian Pyramid (Watch It Grow)*. Time Life Education, 1997.
MacAulay, David, *Pyramid*. Graphia, 1982.

WEBSITES

www.brainboxx.co.uk/a4_resource/pages/history/egyptians.htm
egypt.mrdonn.org/
www.childrensuniversity.manchester.ac.uk/interactives/history/egypt/egyptianmap/
www.neok12.com/Ancient-Egypt.htm

INDEX

Cover: *Ra and Usir sit on thrones, fittingly, since Ra rules aboveground and Usir rules below. In front of each stands a challenger. Aset nearly killed Ra with the snakebite. Set did kill Usir.*

p. 11 Ra: *Ra's first eye felt betrayed when Ra took a second. But Ra, ever resourceful, turned that old eye into a cobra and put her on the front of his crown, where she felt important again.*

p. 31 Set: *The god Set appeared as a mix of parts from different animals: aardvark, jackal, donkey. Over time, he came to be viewed as increasingly evil. Perhaps this conglomeration reflects the lack of peace within him.*

p. 39 Aset: *Aset loved lotuses, the symbol of Upper Egypt. Usir loved papyrus reeds, the symbol of Lower Egypt, especially where the Nile flows into the sea. Together they made the perfect ruling couple for all Egypt.*

p. 63 Usir: *Usir's skin was fish green. But that green signaled the annual hope of a good growing season and harvest. Usir died and then was resurrected, like the earth each year in springtime.*

p. 69 Nebet Hut: *Nebet Hut's arms here form an empty cradle. She longed for a child. But then she got to hold Inpu, then Heru Sa Aset, and finally the newborns of the women she helped through childbirth.*

p. 75 Heru Sa Aset: *Heru Sa Aset grew up in the Nile delta reeds, where his mother hid him to protect him from his wicked uncle, Set, who for many years was the headache of his life.*

p. 81 Inpu: *Inpu loved the stealthy ways of the desert dogs. He followed them and soon his head looked like theirs, only black. Sometimes he took the form of a canine completely.*

p. 87 Tefnut: *Tefnut was moisture itself, the gentle dampness in a breeze, the welcome rain in the middle of a hot spell. Without her, Egypt would have been dry as a bone, crisp as a fire.*

p. 101 Tehuti: *Tehuti was expansive. He was the helmsman of Ra's boats, he gave wise advice to gods who were in trouble, and he taught humans to write and to understand the science of the earth and the skies.*

p. 107 Heru Wer: *Heru Wer is shown here in sphinx form, with the traditional body of a lion. Other sphinx forms have the head of a pharaoh, and some also have the wings of a falcon.*

p. 113 Hut Heru: *Hut Heru was known for her turquoise necklace, the menat, that made a soothing swoosh when she danced, always graceful, like the whispery sound of a breeze passing through papyrus reeds.*

p. 119 Sekhmet: *When Hut Heru was filled with rage, she took the form of Sekhmet and attacked as a lioness. She defended the honor of Amun-Ra against the hateful rumors of the humans.*

p. 127 Nit: *Nit was among the most ancient dieties, and she reflected aspects of many other gods and goddesses. But mostly she was known as a creator; some say she wove the whole world into being.*

p. 135 Khnum: *Khnum was a potter. Some say Ra took Khnum's form when he created all life, using clay as the medium. He also had many wives, so he appeared with the head of a strong, fertile ram.*

p. 141 Sobek: *Sobek was a crocodile in head and heart, and often in his whole body. The people still loved him, though, because he was the lord of the Nile, which was the very pulse of their livelihood.*

p. 149 Bastet: *Bastet was worshipped as a protector against evil spirits and diseases. But she was also simply a kitty, and Egyptians kept cats as favored pets from the Middle Kingdom on.*

p. 156 Funeral Rites: *Although mummification was a sacred ritual, in fact, not all Egyptians' bodies received it. Instead, the mummies that have been found so far are of rich humans and their animals, mostly cats.*

p. 163 Imhotep: *Imhotep was an ordinary human by birth. But he was extraordinary in intellect as a physician, an architect, and an engineer, so he became extraordinary in Egyptian history, rising to the status of a god.*

Published by the National Geographic Society

John M. Fahey,
Chairman of the Board and Chief Executive Officer

Declan Moore,
Executive Vice President; President, Publishing and Travel

Melina Gerosa Bellows,
Executive Vice President; Chief Creative Officer,
  Books, Kids, and Family

Prepared by the Book Division

Hector Sierra,
Senior Vice President and General Manager

Nancy Laties Feresten,
Senior Vice President, Kids Publishing and Media

Jay Sumner,
Director of Photography, Children's Publishing

Jennifer Emmett,
Vice President, Editorial Director, Children's Books

Eva Absher-Schantz,
Design Director, Kids Publishing and Media

R. Gary Colbert, *Production Director*

Jennifer A. Thornton, *Director of Managing Editorial*

Staff for This Book

Priyanka Lamichhane, *Project Editor*

David M. Seager, *Art Director*

Lori Epstein, *Senior Photo Editor*

Ariane Szu-Tu, *Editorial Assistant*

Callie Broaddus, *Design Production Assistant*

Hillary Moloney, *Associate Photo Editor*

Carl Mehler, *Director of Maps*

Stuart Armstrong, *Map Art*

Martin Walz, *Map Research and Production*

Grace Hill, *Associate Managing Editor*

Joan Gossett, *Production Editor*

Lewis R. Bassford, *Production Manager*

Susan Borke, *Legal and Business Affairs*

Production Services

Phillip L. Schlosser, *Senior Vice President*

Chris Brown, Vice President, *NG Book Manufacturing*

Rachel Faulise, *Manager*

Darrick McRae, *Imaging Technician*

The National Geographic Society is one of the world's largest
nonprofit scientific and educational organizations. Founded in
1888 to "increase and diffuse geographic knowledge," the Society's
mission is to inspire people to care about the planet. It reaches
more than 400 million people worldwide each month through its
official journal, *National Geographic,* and other magazines; National
Geographic Channel; television documentaries; music; radio;
films; books; DVDs; maps; exhibitions; live events; school
publishing programs; interactive media; and merchandise.
National Geographic has funded more than 10,000 scientific
research, conservation, and exploration projects and supports an
education program promoting geographic literacy.

For more information, please visit www.nationalgeographic.com,
call 1-800-NGS LINE (647-5463),
or write to the following address:
National Geographic Society
1145 17th Street N.W.
Washington, D.C. 20036-4688 U.S.A.

Visit us online at
nationalgeographic.com/books

For librarians and teachers:
ngchildrensbooks.org

More for kids from National Geographic:
kids.nationalgeographic.com

For information about special discounts for bulk purchases, please
contact National Geographic Books Special Sales:
ngspecsales@ngs.org

For rights or permissions inquiries, please contact
National Geographic Books Subsidiary Rights:
ngbookrights@ngs.org

Hardcover ISBN: 978-1-4263-1380-6
Reinforced Library Edition ISBN: 978-1-4263-1381-3

Printed in the United States of America

13/RRDW-CML/2